SIDE by SIDE

ACTIVITY WORKBOOK

Second Edition

4

Steven J. Molinsky
Bill Bliss

Contributing Authors

Elizabeth Handley / Linda Michon

Longman

Editorial/production supervision: Janet Johnston
Art supervision: Karen Salzbach
Manufacturing buyer: Peter Havens
Cover design: Kenny Beck

Illustrated by Richard E. Hill

Printed in the United States of America

20 19 18 17 16 15

ISBN 0-13-811845-0

CONTENTS

1 Passive Voice 1

2 Noun/Adjective/Adverb Review:
  Count/Non-Count Nouns
  Comparative of Adjectives
  Superlative of Adjectives
  Comparative of Adverbs 11

3 Embedded Questions 23

4 Perfect Modals:
  Should Have
  Must Have
  Might Have
  May Have
  Could Have 33

5 Conditional:
  Present Real (If _____ Will)
  Present Unreal (If _____ Would)
Hope-Clauses 47

6 Present Unreal Conditional
  (continued)
  Wish-Clauses 60

7 Past Unreal Conditional (If _____
  Would Have)
  Wish-Clauses (continued) 69

8 Reported Speech
  Sequence of Tenses 84

9 Tag Questions
  Emphatic Sentences 101

10 Review:
  Verb Tenses
  Conditionals
  Gerunds 112

Tape Scripts for Listening Exercises 130

Correlation Key 133

A. YOU DECIDE: *At the Museum*

1. This car (drive) ___was___ ___driven___

   by the famous sports car driver ....

   ....

   It (make) _____ _____ by the

   ....

   Company in ....
   (year)

2. This airplane (fly) _____ _____

   by ....

   in ..... It (design) _____
   (year)

   _____ by ....

   ....

3. These earrings (wear) _____ _____

   by the famous actress ....

   ....

   They (give) _____ _____ to the
   museum by her granddaughter.

4. This strange machine (invent) _____

   _____ in ....
   (year)

   Unfortunately, it (ride) _____ _____
   only two or three times because it was
   very dangerous.

5. These photographs (take) _____

   _____ by ....

   .... when he/she

   was only 15 years old.   They (leave) ____

   _____ in an old shoe box where they

   (forget) _____ _____ for
   many years.

6. This letter (write) _____ _____ ___

   by ....

   to ....,

   but it (send) _____ never _____.

   It (find) _____ _____ recently
   between the pages of an old book.

(continued)   1

7. This is one of ....'s early operas. It (compose) _____ _____ in ...., and

(year)

it (sing) _____ _____ for the

first time in ....

(year)

8. This impressive bridge (build) _____ _____ in ....

(city)

more than 300 years ago. It (begin) _____ _____ in 1520, and it (finish) _____ until 1600.

9. This portrait ....

. . . .

. . . .

. . . .

. . . .

B. IT'S TOO LATE

Susan is a kind and generous person, but she's a little lazy. She wants to help her friends and family, but she never thinks about helping them until it's too late.

1. I'll be happy to make dinner tonight.

Thank you, Susan. But _it's_ already _been made_ .

2. Can I type your English composition for you?

That's very nice of you. But _____ already _____.

3. Should I write the last few invitations?

Thanks a lot. But _____ already _____.

4. I'll be glad to fix Sally's broken toy.

That's very kind of you. But _____ already _____.

5. Do you want me to hang up your new portrait?

I guess you haven't looked in the living room. _____ already _____.

6. I'll iron the clothes today.

That's nice, dear. But _____ already _____.

7. I think I'll take down the party decorations.

Don't bother. _____ already _____.

C. NOTHING IS READY

> clean the bedrooms
> sweep the porch
> make the salad
> feed the dog
> put the children to bed

A. What are we going to do? All our friends will be arriving soon, and nothing is ready. The

bedrooms _haven't been cleaned_ . The porch _____. The
  1   2

salad _____. The dog _____.
  3   4

And the children _____ to bed. I'm really upset.
                            5

B. Don't worry. Everything will be okay. We still have some time.

3

D. AT THE HOSPITAL

> take Mr. Nelson's blood pressure
> give Mrs. Blake her medicine
> tell Miss Burns about her operation
> send Mr. Warren home

A. How have all the patients been this morning? Have there been any problems?

B. Everything is fine, Doctor.

A. How is Mr. Nelson? _Has_ his blood pressure _been taken_ yet?

1   2

B. Yes, it has. And it wasn't as high as it was yesterday.

A. That's good. _____ Mrs. Blake _____ her medicine?

3   4

B. Yes, she has. And we'll give her some more in another hour.

A. Miss Burns looks upset. _____ she _____ about her operation?

5   6

B. Yes. I explained everything to her, and I think she understands.

A. Is Mr. Warren ready to leave the hospital?

B. He's MORE than ready! _____ already _____ home!

7   8

E. CAN WE LEAVE SOON?

> make the beds
> put away the laundry
> do the dishes
> take out the garbage

A. Can we leave soon?

B. I think so. All the beds _have been made_ , and the laundry _____

      1

  _____ .

2

A. Great!

B. Wait a minute! _____ the dishes _____ ?

3   4

A. No, they haven't. But don't worry about it. I'll do them right away.

B. And now that I think of it, _____ the garbage _____ ?

5   6

A. I'm not sure. Why don't I go and see?

Listen and fill in the missing words.

Ernest Hemingway is considered _____ _____ _____ _____ important modern
                                 1   2   3   4
American writers.   He has _____ six novels and _____ than _____ short
                               5   6   7
stories.   He has also written many _____ and newspaper _____.
                                         8   9
Hemingway's books are lively and _____. They are full of fighting,
                                          10
_____, _____, love, and war.   Hemingway's _____ _____ also
           11   12   13   14
lively and exciting.

When he was a _____ _____ _____ student,
                     15   16   17
Hemingway _____ _____, _____, and _____ for the
              18   19   20   21
school newspaper.   He _____ _____ from home when he was _____ _____
                             22   23   24   25
_____, but he returned and _____ high school in _____.   He never _____
   26   27   28   29
to _____.
         30
Hemingway _____ _____ _____ in World War I, but he
                 31   32   33
_____ _____ _____ the army.   Instead, he went to the war as _____ ambulance
   34   35   36   37
_____ and _____ badly _____.
        38   39   40
In _____ Hemingway went to Paris and _____ _____
       41   42   43
seriously.   He _____ there _____ _____ years.   His _____ novel *The*
                       44   45   46   47
Sun Also Rises _____ _____ when he was _____ _____ Paris.
                     48   49   50   51
It _____ him very _____.
         52   53
In _____ Hemingway _____ _____ Spain as a journalist to write
       54   55   56
_____ the _____ Civil War.
         57   58
In _____ he _____ to Europe and wrote _____
       59   60   61
articles about World War II.   He _____ in the _____ _____ the
                                         62   63   64
Second World War, but it's believed that he did more _____ than
                                                              65
_____, just the same.
         66

Answer in complete sentences.

1. What are Hemingway's novels about? _____

_____

2. What was Hemingway interested in when he was in high school? _____

_____

3. Why couldn't Hemingway fight in World War I? _____

4. What did he do instead? _____

5. Where was Hemingway living when he wrote his first novel? _____

_____

6. Why did Hemingway go to Spain in 1937? _____

_____

7. What did he do in 1944? _____

_____

G. A ROBBERY

Mr. and Mrs. Wilson (rob) _____*were*_____ _____*robbed*_____ last month. Their TV, their
                              1   2

cassette player, and all their living room furniture (take) _____ _____.
                                                              3   4

In fact, nothing (leave) _____ _____ in the living room but the rug.
                            5   6

Fortunately, Mrs. Wilson's gold necklace (take) _____ _____. She was
                                                    7   8

glad because it (give) had been _____ to her by her grandmother many years ago.
                                    9

The thief (see) _____ _____ driving away from the house in a truck.
                   10   11

The neighbors called the police, and the man (arrest) _____ _____. He
                                                          12   13

(send) _____ _____ to jail for five years.
          14   15

A day after the robbery, the living room furniture, the cassette player, and the TV (return)

_____ _____. The sofa (rip) had _____ _____,
   16   17   18   19

but everything else was okay.

6

H. YOU DECIDE: *A Famous Writer*

.... is a talented writer.   She has written many beautiful poems and
                              1

short stories.   Her poems (translated) _____*have*_____ _____*been*_____ _____*translated*_____
                                                    2   3   4

into French, German, and .... Her short stories are often (see) _____
                                          5   6

in magazines.

Ms. .... started to write when she was .... years old.
            7   8

She (give) _____ _____ a book of poetry for her birthday, and she knew right away that she
           9   10

wanted to be a writer.

In 1968 she sent some of her poems to " ...." Magazine, but these early
                                                              11

poems (reject) _____ all _____. Ms. .... was
                     12   13   14

disappointed, but she continued to write.   Finally, in 1971, several of her poems (accept)

_____ _____ by " ...." Magazine.
      15   16   17

It took many years before Ms. ....'s poetry (appreciate) _____
                                              18   19

_____.   At first, her poems (consider) _____ _____
       20   21   22

strange because they were new and different, and they (understand) _____ not easily
                                                                                  23

_____.   Most people couldn't figure them out.   Today, of course, Ms.
       24

.... (respect) is highly _____ by writers all over the world.
          25   26

In 1975 she wrote her most famous short story, called " ...." A year
                                                                                27

later, it (make) _____ _____ into a successful movie.   Since then, she has
                        28   29

written three other short stories that (make) _____ _____ _____ into
                                                          30   31   32

movies.

In 1978 Ms. .... (hurt) _____ badly _____ in a car
                  33   34   35

accident.   She wrote about this terrible accident in a short story called "Driving On."

In 1987 Ms. .... (choose) _____ _____ best writer
                  36   37   38

of the year.   She (invite) _____ _____ to read her poetry at the White
                                   39   40

House in Washington, D.C.

I. WHAT ARE THEY SAYING?

build	carve	feed	hide	promote	repair	take in	tell	wash

1. Why are you taking the subway to work?

   My car was in an accident, and __it's__ still _____being repaired_____.

2. When can we eat the turkey?

   In just a few minutes. _____ right now.

3. Should I pick up my suit at the tailor's?

   Not yet. _____ still _____.

4. Is Louis going to quit his job?

   No.   He's decided to stay because _____.

5. Can I open my eyes?

   Not yet.   The presents _____ still _____.

6. What happened to the shirt I wore yesterday?

   _____.   It was very dirty.

7. Little Susie hasn't eaten since breakfast.

   Don't worry. _____ right now.

8. We won't have to drive over this old bridge much longer.

   That's right.   A new bridge _____ nearby.

9. Has Robert heard about his brother's accident?

   I think _____ right now.

J. A COLLEGE TOUR

I'm glad you've all come to visit our college.   I hope that many of you will enroll next year.

First, let's visit some of our classrooms.   In this room, students (teach) ___*are*___ ___*being*___
₁ ₂

___*taught*___ French.   Here at Greenville College, we believe that all students (teach) should
₃

___ _____ to speak a foreign language.
₄ ₅

The students in the next room are studying history.   History classes are usually very lively,

but today the students (give) _____ _____ _____ an examination.
₆ ₇ ₈

This room is a science classroom.   You can stay for awhile and listen.   I'm sure many

interesting ideas (discuss) _____ _____ _____ right now.
₉ ₁₀ ₁₁

In a little while, we're going to see the cafeteria where all the school food (prepare) is

_____.   We believe that young people (feed) should _____ _____ good
₁₂ ₁₃ ₁₄

nutritious food.   That's why we've planted the vegetable garden you see next to the cafeteria.   The

vegetables that our students are eating today (grow) _____ _____ _____ in our
₁₅ ₁₆ ₁₇

garden.

The next stop on the tour will be the college hospital.   It (build) _____ _____ last
₁₈ ₁₉

year and is the school's most modern building.   Patients at the college hospital (take) are

_____ care of by excellent nurses and doctors who (train) _____ _____
₂₀ ₂₁ ₂₂

_____ at the best universities.
₂₃

Students from Greenville College are well prepared for life.   Many of our former students

(hire) _____ _____ _____ by fine companies where they've (give)
₂₄ ₂₅ ₂₆

_____ _____ important jobs.
₂₇ ₂₈

We hope you've enjoyed your tour of Greenville College.

K. WHAT DOES IT MEAN?

Put a circle around the appropriate answer.

1. I've got to take in my suit.
   a. It's too small.
   b. It's too big.
   c. It's too hot.

2. We need an ambulance right away.
   a. We're having problems with our apartment.
   b. We're trying to repair something.
   c. Aunt Gertrude just had another heart attack.

3. Mr. Smith was promoted.
   a. He was hired.
   b. He was fired.
   c. He was given a more important job.

4. I'm carving the chicken.
   a. I'm putting it away.
   b. I'm slicing it.
   c. I'm cooking it.

5. I have to sweep the kitchen.
   a. The floor is dirty.
   b. The windows are dirty.
   c. The sink is dirty.

6. Tom is choosing a new suit.
   a. He's dropping off a new suit.
   b. He's picking out a new suit.
   c. He's taking in a new suit.

7. I just woke up the children.
   a. I took them for a walk.
   b. They were waiting for me at the bus stop.
   c. They were sleeping.

8. John's will has just been rewritten.
   a. He's going to pick it up at the law office.
   b. He's going to pick it up at the book store.
   c. He's going to pick it up at the high school.

9. Alice was rejected by Greenville College.
   a. She'll be going there next year.
   b. She was turned down.
   c. She's been studying there for four years.

10. You'll be allowed to vote when you're 18 years old.
    a. You'll be required to vote.
    b. You'll want to vote.
    c. You'll be permitted to vote.

11. We're waiting for the mailman.
    a. He's going to fix the washing machine.
    b. He's going to paint the porch.
    c. He's going to bring us some important letters.

12. Ellen always wears beautiful jewelry.
    a. She wears beautiful jackets and skirts.
    b. She wears beautiful shoes and gloves.
    c. She wears beautiful bracelets and earrir

13. Larry was robbed last week.
    a. He was sent to jail.
    b. His TV was taken.
    c. He was given some new clothes.

14. My feet are frozen.
    a. They're very cold.
    b. They're tired.
    c. They're dirty.

15. Mrs. Williams is hiding her money.
    a. She can't find her money.
    b. She's spending her money.
    c. She's putting her money where nobody can find it.

16. Bill is sitting on the porch.
    a. He's in the park.
    b. He's at home.
    c. He's sitting on a car.

17. Lois is going to Paris on business.
    a. She's taking her vacation in Paris.
    b. She's taking a bus tour of Paris.
    c. Her company is sending her to Paris.

18. I can hear the church bells.
    a. They're singing.
    b. They're ringing.
    c. They're talking.

A. WHAT'S THE WORD?

1. Mr. and Mrs. Hardy are moving because their old neighborhood has too [much / (many)] unfriendly people, too [much / many] fast cars, and too [much / many] noise.

2. I love your recipe for soup. It's not as spicy as mine. I don't think you use as [much / many] onions or as [much / many] pepper as I do.

3. Poor Jim! He did poorly on his English examination because he took too [much / many] time to think about his answers and made too [much / many] mistakes.

4. Emily has to find a new job. She was fired from her old job because her boss said she used too [much / many] typing paper, too [much / many] envelopes, and too [much / many] ink. He also said she drank too [much / many] coffee and made too [much / many] telephone calls to her friends.

5. Since you went to cooking school your cheese omelettes are much better. I don't think you use as [much / many] eggs, as [much / many] cheese, or as [much / many] salt as you did before.

6. Paul always complains about his high school. He says that taking too [much / many] books home from school gives him a backache, going to too [much / many] noisy classes gives him an earache, and doing too [much / many] homework gives him a headache.

(continued)

7. I really hate to use the bathroom after my brother Edward in the morning. He always uses too

much
many

toothpaste, too

much
many

soap, too

much
many

shampoo, and too

much
many

hot water.

There's never anything left for me!

8. Mrs. Thompson is disappointed because the fruitcake that she baked last night wasn't

successful. She thinks she used too

much
many

flour, too

much
many

baking soda, too

much
many

raisins, and too

much
many

nuts.

9. I certainly don't want your job! You're much too busy. You have to type too

much
many

letters

and make too

much
many

appointments. And you have to work too

much
many

evenings a week.

Your job is too

much
many

work for me!

10. Albert hates his new diet because he can't eat as

much
many

potatoes, as

much
many

rice, as

much
many

butter, or as

much
many

snack foods as before.

11. Mrs. Harris isn't going to send her son to the store anymore. When she asked him to get some

laundry detergent, he got too

much
many

. When she asked him to buy some eggs, he bought too

much
many

. Later, when she sent him to get some window cleaner, he brought back too

much
many

.

Finally, when Mrs. Harris sent her son to get some vitamins and he got too

much
many

again,

Mrs. Harris decided to go to the store herself!

B. THEY COULDN'T UNDERSTAND WHY!

1. Sharon didn't feel very well when she got up this morning.   She had a terrible stomachache, and she couldn't understand why.   After all, last night at the party she had eaten only:

| a little |
| a few |

1. _____a little_____ chocolate cake
2. _____ chicken and rice
3. _____ crackers
4. _____ Swiss cheese
5. _____ strawberry ice cream
6. _____ pizza

7. _____ french fries
8. _____ cookies
9. ....
10. ....
11. ....
12. ....

Sharon didn't think she had eaten too much at all!

2. Carlos is planning to visit his grandparents in Madrid for a month.   When he finished packing his suitcase this morning, he wasn't able to lift it, and he couldn't understand why.   After all, he had put in only:

| a little |
| a few |

1. _____ shirts
2. _____ suits and ties
3. _____ soap and shampoo
4. _____ jackets and sweaters
5. _____ Spanish dictionaries
6. _____ candy and perfume for his grandmother and wine for his grandfather

7. _____ newspapers and magazines to read on the plane
8. _____ presents for his relatives in Madrid
9. ....
10. ....
11. ....
12. ....

Carlos didn't think he had packed too much at all!

13

Listen and put a circle around the correct answer.

1. a. No. Not too much.
    b. No. Not too many. *(circled)*

2. a. No. Not too much.
    b. No. Not too many.

3. a. Just a little.
    b. Just a few.

4. a. Yes. But just a little.
    b. Yes. But just a few.

5. a. No. Not too much.
    b. No. Not too many.

6. a. Just a little, please.
    b. Just a few, please.

7. a. No. Not too much.
    b. No. Not too many.

8. a. No. Not too much.
    b. No. Not too many.

9. a. Just a little.
    b. Just a few.

10. a. Just a little.
     b. Just a few.

11. a. Yes. But just a little.
     b. Yes. But just a few.

12. a. Sure. But not too much.
     b. Sure. But not too many.

D. MY FAVORITE VEGETABLE SOUP

much	many	little	few

A. Here's how you make my favorite vegetable soup. You start with some butter.

B. How ___much___ ?
  1

A. Just a _____ .
  2

B. And then?

A. Then you slice a _____ onions and cook them in butter.
  3

B. How _____ onions?
  4

A. As _____ as you like.
  5

B. And then?

A. Then you add a _____ water.
  6

B. How _____ ?
  7

A. Not too _____ . Just a
  8
_____ cups.
  9

B. And after that?

A. You add a little . . . . ,
  10
a little . . . . , a few
  11
. . . . , and a few
  12
. . . .
  13

B. How long do you cook the soup?

A. Not too long. Just a _____ hours.
  14

B. Thanks for the recipe. I'll try it soon.

E. WHICH APARTMENT IS BETTER?

Donald and Gloria are looking for a place to live. Last week they saw an apartment on Grant Street that Donald liked very much. This week they're looking at an apartment on Brighton Boulevard that Gloria likes better.

GLORIA: The living room in the Grant Street apartment is so small, and this one is much

(large) _larger_ . Also, the kitchen in the Grant Street apartment is so dark, and this
1

one is much (light) _____.
2

DONALD: That's true. But the Grant Street apartment is cheap, and this one is much

(expensive) _____.
3

GLORIA: No wonder! That's because the Grant Street apartment is old and ugly, and this one

is much (new) _____ and (pretty) _____. The Grant Street
4   5

yard is so little, and this yard is much (big) _____.
6

DONALD: But don't you think the superintendent at the Brighton Boulevard apartment is lazy?

I'm sure the Grant Street superintendent is much (energetic) _____.
7

And I think the Brighton Boulevard landlord is stingy. The one on Grant Street is

much (generous) _____.
8

GLORIA: You might be right. But Grant Street is so narrow and dirty, and Brighton

Boulevard is much (wide) _____ and (clean) _____.
9   10

DONALD: I agree. But the Brighton Boulevard neighbors are so unfriendly, and the Grant

Street neighbors are much (hospitable) _____. Don't you think
11

that living on Brighton Boulevard is going to be boring? I'm sure that living on

Grant Street will be much (interesting) _____.
12

GLORIA: Hmm. What do you think we should do?

DONALD: I don't know. I guess we should look at the apartment on School Street before we
decide.

F. THE BEST/WORST EVENING WE'VE EVER HAD!

Last night my sister Frieda and I went out to a restaurant for dinner and to the ballet.

I thought the restaurant was wonderful, but my sister thought it was the (bad) _____worst_____ restaurant she had ever been to.   I thought the food was delicious and exciting, but Frieda thought it was the (plain) _____ food she had ever eaten.

After dinner, we took a taxi to the theater.   I thought the taxi was fast, but my sister thought it was the (slow) _____ taxi she had ever taken.   I thought the taxi driver was polite and careful. Frieda thought he was the (impolite) _____ and the (dangerous) _____ taxi driver she had ever met.

At the ballet, my sister thought the dancers were clumsy, but I thought they were the (graceful) _____ and the (talented) _____ dancers I had ever seen.   Frieda thought the theater was ugly, but I thought it was the (beautiful) _____ theater I had ever seen.   I thought the seats were soft and comfortable, but my sister thought they were the (hard) _____ and the (uncomfortable) _____ seats she had ever sat in.   Frieda thought the ballet was boring, but I thought it was the (interesting) _____ ballet I had ever been to.

My sister Frieda complained so much that she made me have a terrible time, but I really think SHE had the (bad) _____ time of all.

G. VINCENT'S FRUIT MARKET

> Vincent's Fruit Market is known for its
> *ripe pears,*
> *delicious oranges,*
> *fresh grapefruits,* and
> *shiny apples!*

Many people have stopped buying fruit at their neighborhood supermarket and have started to shop at Vincent's Fruit Market.   Why?   Because they've learned that at Vincent's:

(1) _____*the pears*_____ are _____*riper*_____,

(2) _____ are _____,

(3) _____ are _____, and

(4) _____ are _____.

In fact, everybody agrees that Vincent's Fruit Market has:

(5) _____*the ripest pears*_____,

(6) _____,

(7) _____, and

(8) _____ in town!

H. GREEN'S GARDEN SHOP

> Do you want to have
> *tall trees,*
> *beautiful flowers,*
> *sturdy plants,* and
> *red tomatoes?*

Green's Garden Shop is having the biggest sale they've ever had on *Grow-More Plant Food.*   Use *Grow-More Plant Food* for just one week, and

your (1) _____*trees*_____ will grow much _____*taller*_____,

your (2) _____ will be much _____,

your (3) _____ will get _____, and

your (4) _____ will be much _____.

Use *Grow-More Plant Food* for just one MONTH, and you'll have

(5) _____*the tallest trees*_____,

(6) _____,

(7) _____, and

(8) _____ in your neighborhood!

I. THE GOLD STAR BUSINESS SCHOOL

Do you think that getting a better job is difficult?   Well, it won't be difficult at all if you come to the Gold Star Business School.   We'll help you get a better job much (easily) _____*more easily*_____
1

and much (quickly) _____ than you think.
2

Our fine teachers will teach you to read much (fast) _____, write much (neatly)
3

_____, and answer the telephone much (politely) _____
4   5

than you do now.   Our teachers will also prepare you to make business decisions much (carefully)

_____ and get along with your boss much (good) _____.
6   7

Before you finish our classes, you'll be able to hire employees much (easily) _____

_____ and complete your income tax forms much (accurately) _____
8

_____ than you do now.
9

And that's not all!   Our teachers can also give you advice about how to work much

(energetically) _____ and look at life much (enthusiastically)
10

_____.
11

You'll find that getting a new job is really easy with the help of the Gold Star Business
School!

I just finished studying at the Gold Star Business School, and now I'm a NEW PERSON!   After

just two weeks, I can ....

....

....

....

....

18

J. WHAT ARE THEY SAYING?

1. Now that Jack is a taxi driver, he doesn't drive _as carefully as_ he used to.

   I know. He was a much more careful driver when he was driving an ambulance.

2. Are you as accurate as your boss?

   Actually, I type much _____ than he does.

3. Bill sings the national anthem very _____.

   That's true. But you should hear his sister. Her voice is even more beautiful.

4. I've heard that Martha is a very graceful dancer.

   So have I. But now that she's broken her leg, she doesn't dance _____ she used to.

5. That was _____ concert we've ever been to.

   You're right! I didn't know it was going to be so bad.

6. I'm really jealous. I don't play basketball _____ the other players on my team.

   That's not true! You play much better than they do!

7. Everyone says that Michael works so hard!

   Well, they're right. He's _____ worker in our bakery.

8. Sally's Russian is very fluent.

   I know. And ever since she took her vacation in Russia last summer, she speaks even _____ than she used to.

9. Your puppy is getting so big. Is he as friendly as he used to be?

   Oh, yes. As he gets _____, he also gets _____!

10. Have you been answering the questions in Workbook 4 as carefully as you did in Workbook 3?

    Of course I have. I've been answering them much _____.

19

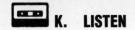

K. LISTEN

Listen to each word and then say it.

bother:	both:	busy:	boss:
1. this	1. think	1. music	1. sink
2. father	2. birthday	2. doesn't	2. disappointed
3. they're	3. Theodore	3. days	3. guess
4. that	4. throat	4. easy	4. serious
5. weather	5. Martha	5. because	5. cost
6. neither	6. teeth	6. loves	6. looks

L. WHAT ARE _ _EY _AYING?

Fill in the missing letters and then read the conversation aloud.

A. My bro_ _er _ _eodore doe_n't _ _ink he can go to _ _e _ _eater wi_ _ u_

_ _is _aturday becau_e he ha_ a _ore _ _roat.

B. Ano_ _er sore throat? _ _at's terrible. Didn't he ju_t get over one la_t _ _ursday?

A. _ _at's right. Believe it or not, _ _is is _ _e _ _ird _ore _ _roat he'_ had _ _is

mon_ _. My poor bro_ _er alway_ get_ _ick when _ _e wea_ _er i_ very cold.

B. I hope it i_n't _eriou_ _ _is time.

A. I don't _ _ink _o. _ _eodore _ays hi_ _ore _ _roat isn't bo_ _ering him too much.

But bo_ _ my mo_ _er and fa_ _er _ay he'll have to re_t in bed for a few day_

anyway. _ _ey're worried becau_e he i_n't eating any_ _ing, and _ _ey don't _ _ink

he look_ very heal_ _y.

B. _ _en I gue_ _ he won't be going to _ _e _unday concert ei_ _er.

A. Probably not. And he'_ very di_appointed. He really love_ cla_ _ical mu_ic.

B. Well, I'm _orry our plan_ fell _ _rough. Plea_ e tell _ _eodore I hope he feel_

better _oon. Oh, I almo_t forgot. My little si_ter Mar_ _a is having a _mall

bir_ _day celebration today at _ _ree _ _irty. Would you like to come?

A. Ye_, of cour_e. _ _ank you very much.

A. Complete the sentences.

(graceful)   1. Since I started taking dancing lessons, I've been dancing much ____*more*____

_____*gracefully*_____ . Soon I'll be _____*the most graceful*_____

dancer in my class.

(experienced)   2. I'm going to call Mr. Chen. He's _____ plumber I
can find.

(accurate)   3. Bill doesn't type _____ as he used to because he's
stopped paying attention.

(sturdy)   4. I really like your new briefcase. It's _____ than mine.

(good)   5. That's _____ book I've ever read.

(energetic)   6. Taking vitamins will help you work much _____.

(bad)   7. I had a very _____ day yesterday. It was _____ day
I've ever had.

(nutritious)   8. My doctor recommends eating fruit because it's _____
than candy.

(fast)   9. If you want to get home before 3:00, you'll have to work much _____.

(enthusiastic)   10. Tim lives life _____ than any other person
I know.

(good)   11. I don't play the piano _____ as Ronald does, but I play

_____ than Walter.

(clear)   12. Our math teacher explained our last lesson very _____.

(quick)   13. The Gold Star Business School will help you get a job much _____
than you think.

(tall)   14. Sally is growing up. She's much _____ she was
last year.

B. Fill in the blanks with the passive voice.

(write)   Ex. This poem ___*was*___ ____*written*____ in 1988.

(build)   1. Our beautiful new cafeteria _____ _____ last year.

(repair)   2. I can't drive my car to work. _____ still _____ _____.

(give)   3. Helen _____ _____ _____ a raise twice this year.

(teach)   4. All students should _____ _____ a foreign language.

(do)   5. Nobody has to do the dishes tonight. _____ already _____

_____.

(take in)   6. Your pants aren't ready yet. _____ still _____ _____ _____.

(choose)   7. Miss Taylor _____ _____ best actress of the year in 1968.

(sweep)   8. The porch is very dirty. It _____ _____ _____ yet.

(make)   9. That's a very interesting novel. I really think it should _____ _____ into a movie.

(send)   10. Mrs. Jones is still in the hospital. She _____ _____ _____ home yet.

(tell)   11. Jim didn't see the accident. _____ _____ _____ about it right now.

C. Listen to each question. Put a circle around the correct answer.

Ex. (a.) Yes, please.   A little.
    b. Yes, please.   A few.

1. a. Yes.   Just a little.
   b. Yes.   Just a few.

2. a. No.   Not too much.
   b. No.   Not too many.

3. a. No.   Not too much.
   b. No.   Not too many.

4. a. Yes, please.   Just a little.
   b. Yes, please.   Just a few.

5. a. No.   Not too much.
   b. No.   Not too many.

6. a. Yes.   But just a little.
   b. Yes.   But just a few.

7. a. Yes.   But not too much.
   b. Yes.   But not too many.

8. a. Take as much as you want.
   b. Take as many as you want.

A. SHE DIDN'T SAY

3

1. Were you just talking to Judy on the phone?

Yes. She called from college.

2. How is she?

Fine.

3. The last time I heard from her, she was looking for an apartment. Where is she living now?

I don't know _where she's living now_. She didn't say.

4. What courses has she been taking?

I have no idea _____. She didn't say.

5. How are her parents?

I'm not sure _____. She didn't say.

6. Well, tell me about her brother. When will he be starting his new job?

I don't know _____. She didn't say.

7. I really miss Judy. When is she going to come to New York?

I'm not sure _____. She didn't say.

8. Well, when will her spring vacation begin?

I don't know _____. She didn't say.

9. Hmm. Who has she been going out with?

I have no idea _____. She didn't say.

10. Why hasn't she written to anyone?

I'm not sure _____. She didn't say.

11. This is RIDICULOUS! I'm going to call Judy back and talk to her myself. What's her telephone number?

I don't know _____. She didn't say.

B. YOU'LL HAVE TO ASK SOMEBODY ELSE

A. Hello, Ivan.   Where have you been?   I haven't seen you all week.

B. I've been in bed with a bad cold, but I'll be back in school on Monday.   Tell me, Jim.   What math homework did we have yesterday?

A. Math homework?   I don't remember _____ *what math homework we had* _____.
   I'm afraid you'll have to ask somebody else.
   1

B. That's okay.   What did we do in French class on Thursday?

A. French class?   I've forgotten _____

   _____.   I guess you'll have to ask somebody else.
   2

B. When do we have to hand in our English compositions?   I haven't finished mine yet.

A. English compositions?   I'm not sure _____

   _____.   You'll have to ask somebody else.
   3

B. How many lessons did we read in geography?

A. Geography?   I can't remember _____

   _____.   You should probably ask somebody else.
   4

B. What homework did Mr. Arnold give us?

A. Homework?   I don't remember _____

   _____.   Can you ask somebody else?
   5

B. What did we write about in history class?

A. History class?   I've forgotten _____

   _____.   Why don't you ask somebody
   else?   6

B. Good-bye, Jim.   Thanks for your help.

24

C. TOO MANY QUESTIONS

A. Grandma, when did you learn to knit?

B. I can't remember _____ *when I learned to knit* _____.
   It was a very long time ago. 1

A. Why doesn't my mother like to knit?

B. I don't know _____.
   You'll have to ask her. 2

A. Grandma, I've been thinking. . . . Why do elephants have long ears?

B. I have no idea _____. 3

A. How do birds learn to fly?

B. I don't know _____. 4

A. Why . . . . ? 5

B. I'm not sure 6

A. Why . . . . ? 7

B. I don't know 8

A. How . . . . ? 9

B. I don't know 10

A. What . . . . ? 11

B. I have no idea 12

A. Grandma?

B. Yes? What did you want to ask me?

A. I can't remember _____. 13

B. That's okay.

D. LISTEN

Listen and complete the sentences.

Ex. I don't know _____ *what you should do* _____.

1. I have no idea _____.

2. I'm not sure _____.

3. I've forgotten _____.

4. I don't know _____.

5. I don't know _____.

6. I'm not sure _____.

7. I have no idea _____.

8. I can't remember _____.

9. I'm not sure _____.

10. I don't remember _____.

E. YOU DECIDE: *What Are They Saying?*

Answer the questions with any vocabulary you wish.

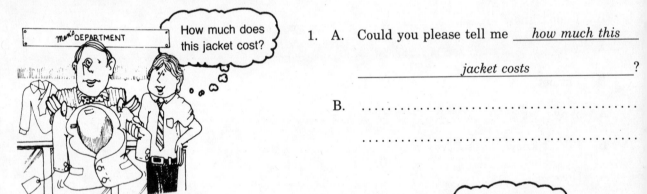

1. A. Could you please tell me ____ *how much this* ____

   _____ *jacket costs* _____ ?

   B. ....

   ....

2. A. Do you know _____

   _____ ?

   B. ....

   ....

26

How long have we been playing?

3. A. Do you have any idea _____

_____ ?

B. ....

....

4. A. Do you by any chance know _____

_____ ?

B. ....

....

Whose watch is this?

When will I be getting out of here?

5. A. Do you have any idea _____

_____ ?

B. ....

....

6. A. Could you please tell me _____

_____ ?

B. ....

....

How can I get to the museum from here?

SUBWAY

What are you learning at school?

7. A. Can you tell Mrs. Johnson _____

_____ ?

B. ....

....

(continued)   27

Why have you been late to work all week?

8. A. Can you tell me _____

_____ ?

B. ....

....

When will my pants be ready?

9. A. Can you tell me _____

_____ ?

B. ....

....

Where can I find a good hotel?

10. A. Could you possibly tell me _____

_____ ?

B. ....

....

Where's the nearest gas station?

11. A. Do you know _____

_____ ?

B. ....

....

Why did you decide to become an actor?

12. A. Could you please tell us _____

_____ ?

B. ....

....

F. RENTING AN APARTMENT

Ask the agent:

1. *Has it been rented yet?*
2. *Is there an elevator in the building?*
3. *Does the kitchen have a dishwasher?*
4. *Are pets allowed?*
5. *Is there a bus stop nearby?*
6. *Does the landlord live in the building?*
7. ....?
8. *Can I see the apartment sometime this afternoon?*

1. I'm calling about the apartment at 39 Beach Street. Could you tell me ____*(if/whether) it's been*____ ____*rented yet*____ ?

   Not yet.   But a lot of people have called.   Would you like to see it?

2. Thank you.   But first I have a few questions.   According to the newspaper, the apartment is on the third floor.   Can you tell me _____ _____ ?

   Yes.   As a matter of fact, there are two elevators.

3. Do you know _____ _____ ?

   I'm sure it does.   It's a very modern kitchen.

4. Can you tell me _____ _____ ?

   I'm not sure.   I'll have to ask the landlord.   He can tell us _____ _____

(continued)

5. Also, do you by any chance

know _____

_____?

Yes. The Central Avenue bus stops at the corner.

6. That's very convenient. Can you also

tell me _____

_____?

Yes, he does. And everybody says he takes very good care of the apartments.

7. And could you please tell

me . . . .

. . . . ?

. . . .

. . . .

8. You've been very helpful. Do you

know _____

_____

_____?

Certainly. Why don't you come by our office at 2:00, and we'll take you there.

📼 **G. LISTEN** **Listen and complete the sentences.**

Ex. I don't know _____ *whether your car will be ready today* . _____

1. I don't know _____

2. I don't know _____

3. I don't know _____

4. I don't know _____

5. I don't know _____

6. I don't know _____

7. I don't know _____

8. I don't know _____

9. I don't know _____

10. I don't know _____

H. YOU DECIDE: *Henry's Vacation*

Ask Mr. Simpson:
1. *How long is the flight to . . . . ?*
2. *Where can I rent a car when I get there?*
3. *Do I need an international driver's license?*
4. *How's the weather in June?*
5. *What tourist sights did you like best?*
6. *Where can I find a good hotel?*
7. *Will I have to speak . . . . all the time?*
8. . . . . ?
9. . . . . ?

1. Hello, Mr. Simpson.   I'm planning

   to fly to . . . . on
   my summer vacation this June.   My
   mother says you've been there
   several times.   Can you tell me

   _____

   _____ ?

   It's . . . . hours.

2. Do you know _____

   _____

   when I get there?

3. Can you tell me _____

   _____

   _____ ?

4. Also, could you tell me _____

   _____

   in June?

(continued)   31

5. I've been reading a little about the tourist sights in ...., and I know I won't be able to see everything. Can you tell me _____ _____ _____ best?

....
....
....
....

6. Do you know _____ _____?

....
....
....

7. I'm a little worried about speaking .... Do you know _____ _____ all the time?

....
....
....

8. Can you also tell me ....?

....
....
....

9. And do you know ....?

....
....
....

10. Thank you, Mr. Simpson. I'm really looking forward to my trip.

I'm sure you'll have a wonderful time. Send me a postcard.

32

A. YOU DECIDE: *Aunt Gertrude's Advice*

should have   shouldn't have

All my life, my Aunt Gertrude has always given me advice.   She started giving me advice when I was a young boy.

1. Mom is really angry because she tripped and fell when she came into my room this morning.

    Well, you should have ....
    ...., you shouldn't
    have ....,
    and you should have ....
    ....

2. Dad is upset because I got a terrible grade on my last composition.

3. By the time I got to Sally's birthday party the other day, everybody had already left.

Aunt Gertrude was still giving me advice as I got older, got married, and had children.

4. My son Brian had terrible nightmares all last night.

5. I'm very upset.   My daughter Maria had a very bad cold last month, and it took her three weeks to get over it.

(continued)

6. I'm really embarrassed. I ran in the marathon last weekend, and I finished LAST!

7. My son Jeffrey borrowed the car and had an accident. HE'S fine, but my car ISN'T!

Even now that I'm retired, Aunt Gertrude STILL gives me advice.

8. I couldn't find my reading glasses all last night!

9. I had a terrible backache the other day after I played baseball with some of the young children in the neighborhood.

10. I took my granddaughter to the symphony last Saturday, and she couldn't stand it!

11. I had to do my will over again. My lawyer couldn't read it!

I can't think of life without Aunt Gertrude's advice.

B. WHAT HAPPENED?

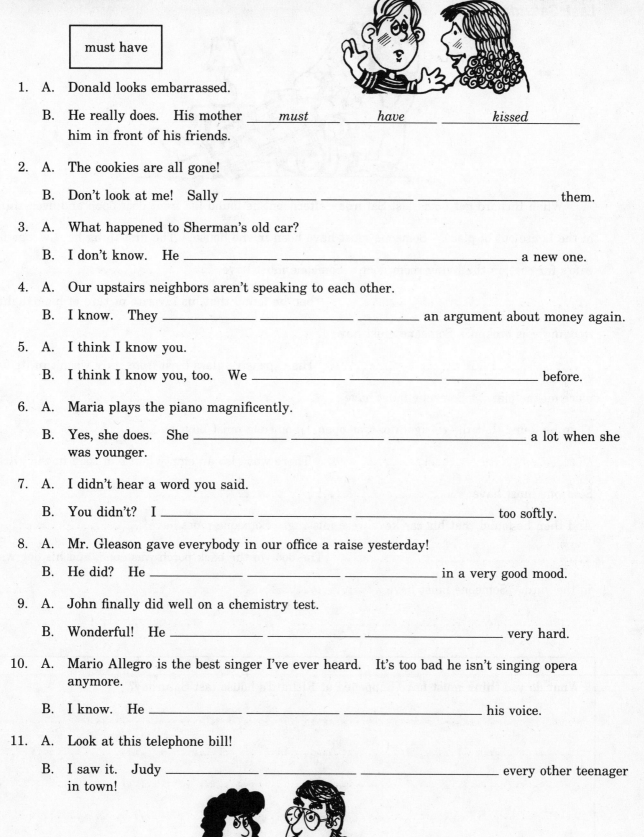

must have

1. A. Donald looks embarrassed.

    B. He really does.   His mother ____*must*____ ____*have*____ ____*kissed*____ him in front of his friends.

2. A. The cookies are all gone!

    B. Don't look at me!   Sally _____ _____ _____ them.

3. A. What happened to Sherman's old car?

    B. I don't know.   He _____ _____ _____ a new one.

4. A. Our upstairs neighbors aren't speaking to each other.

    B. I know.   They _____ _____ _____ an argument about money again.

5. A. I think I know you.

    B. I think I know you, too.   We _____ _____ _____ before.

6. A. Maria plays the piano magnificently.

    B. Yes, she does.   She _____ _____ _____ a lot when she was younger.

7. A. I didn't hear a word you said.

    B. You didn't?   I _____ _____ _____ too softly.

8. A. Mr. Gleason gave everybody in our office a raise yesterday!

    B. He did?   He _____ _____ _____ in a very good mood.

9. A. John finally did well on a chemistry test.

    B. Wonderful!   He _____ _____ _____ very hard.

10. A. Mario Allegro is the best singer I've ever heard.   It's too bad he isn't singing opera anymore.

    B. I know.   He _____ _____ _____ his voice.

11. A. Look at this telephone bill!

    B. I saw it.   Judy _____ _____ _____ every other teenager in town!

C. YOU DECIDE: *What Do You Think Must Have Happened at Richard's House Last Saturday?*

When Richard got home last Saturday afternoon, he found his front door open and everything in the house out of place. Someone must have been in the house! The first thing he saw was his wife's fur coat on the living room floor. Someone must have .... Then he found that his favorite picture of his daughter's wedding was broken. Someone must have ....

.... His expensive glass bowl from Italy wasn't in its usual place on the piano. Someone must have ....

Then he found that the refrigerator was open. Someone must have ....

.... There was also an empty bottle of soda in the kitchen. Someone must have ....

And then he found that his car keys were missing! Someone must have ....

.... The door to the back porch was open, and his dog wasn't in the yard. Someone must have ....

....

What do you think must have happened at Richard's house last Saturday?

....

....

....

....

....

....

D. YOU DECIDE: *What Might Have Happened?*

1. What did your neighbors name their new baby boy?

   I'm not sure. They might have ....

   ...., or they might have ....

   ....

   Didn't they want to name him after the President?

   You're right. Then they must have ....

   ....

2. What did George have for dinner at the restaurant last night?

   I'm not sure. He might have ....

   ...., or he might have ....

   ....

   Didn't you see that tomato sauce all over his tie?

   No, I didn't. He must have ....

   ....

3. Where did Claudia go on her vacation?

   I don't know. She may have ....

   ...., or she may have ....

   ....

   She sent me a picture of herself in front of the Great Wall.

   Then she must have ....

4. Poor Roger! His car wouldn't start this morning. How did he get to work?

I don't know. He might have ....

........................., or he might have ....

....

He asked his sister if her bicycle was working.

Then he must have ....

....

5. Do you know what Barbara's husband got her for her birthday?

No, I don't. He may have ....

........................., or he may have ....

....

She told him she didn't have anything to wear to the Nelsons' party.

Then he must have ....

....

6. Arthur was rejected by the army last September. Do you know why?

Not really. He might have ....

........................., or he might have ....

....

According to his mother, he weighs 300 pounds!

Oh, no! Then he must have ....

....

7.

Why was Harry fired?

I don't know. He might have ....
........................, or he might have ....
....

Whenever I called him at work, they said he wasn't there.

Oh. Then he must have ....
....

8.

Do you know why Mr. Anderson was arrested?

No, but he might have ....
........................, or he might have ....
....

The police found 20 TVs in his basement!

Oh, well. Then he must have ....
....

9.

I wonder what vegetables Edward planted in his garden this spring.

I don't know. He might have ....
........................, or he might have ....
.... He likes them both.

The last three times I went to his house we had carrot juice, carrot soup, carrot cookies, and carrot cake!!

Oh! Then he must have ....
....

E. I DON'T UNDERSTAND IT!

could have

1. I don't understand it.   My son ____could____ ____have____ ____become____ anything he wanted to.   Why did he decide to become a magician?!

2. I don't understand it.   George _____ _____ _____ anybody he wanted to.   Why did he marry Mabel?

3. Those tourists _____ _____ _____ at any restaurant in town.   Why did they eat at Joe's Cafeteria?

4. Gregory _____ _____ _____ any course he wanted to.   I wonder why he's taking first-year French for the fourth time!

5. Tom had an important job interview yesterday.   He _____ _____ _____ any tie he wanted to.   I wonder why he wore the green and yellow striped one with orange polka dots!

6. Michael _____ _____ _____ anything on TV last night.   Why did he watch an old western he had already seen several times before?

7. Mrs. Watson _____ _____ _____ anywhere on her vacation. Nobody can understand why she went to Centerville.

8. Melissa Grant _____ _____ _____ in any play on Broadway. I wonder why she's in this awful play!

9. I can't believe it!   My friend John _____ _____ _____ me a postcard from ANY country he visited on his trip around the world.   But he never sent me anything.

10. Sam _____ _____ _____ any kind of magazine article he wanted to. Why did he write about vacuum cleaners?

11. Professor Jones is a genius.   He _____ _____ _____ any kind of machine he wanted to.   I wonder why he invented a singing typewriter!!

F. THE NIGHT UNCLE BOB WAS ARRESTED

could have	might have	should have
couldn't have	must have	shouldn't have

A. Tell me the story about the night Uncle Bob was arrested.

B. You don't really want to hear that old story again. I _____*must have*_____ told it to you a hundred times!
₁

A. I know. But I'd like to hear it again.

B. Well, all right. I'll never forget the night they arrested your Uncle Bob for stealing a car. As

soon as I heard he was in trouble, I called the police station because I knew he _____
₂

done anything like that. Not your Uncle Bob! He _____ been driving too fast,
₃

or he _____ missed a stop sign, but I just KNEW that he _____
₄ ₅

stolen a car! I knew that the police officer _____ arrested the wrong man.
₆

Later, we found out what really had happened. Your Uncle Bob couldn't find his keys and was
trying to get into his car. The only way he could do that was by breaking the window.

That's when the police arrived. Your Uncle Bob _____ been so impatient. He
₇

_____ called me because I had the keys to his car all the time. He had left them
₈

at my house and _____ forgotten them.
₉

A. That's my favorite story. Thanks for telling it.

G. WHAT'S THE WORD?

could have	might have	should have
couldn't have	must have	shouldn't have

1. I'm so hot! I __*shouldn't*__ __*have*__ worn my winter coat today. I'm sorry I did.

2. Your house looks like new since the fire. You _____ _____ spent a lot of time repairing it.

3. Michael _____ _____ taken us sailing on such a windy day.

   We _____ _____ gotten seasick.

4. It was so dark in my basement that I fell down the stairs. I _____ _____ fixed that broken light.

5. Patty is crazy! She _____ _____ gotten to New York any way she wanted. Why did she hitchhike?

(continued) 41

6. I called Stuart's apartment all night and nobody answered. He _____ _____ gone out.

7. You _____ _____ swept the front porch. It looks so clean.

8. He _____ _____ stolen the car. He was with me all the time.

9. My washing machine is broken. The repairman said I never _____ _____ tried to wash four pairs of sneakers and five pairs of jeans at the same time.

H. WHAT DOES IT MEAN?

Put a circle around the appropriate answer.

1. Roger overslept.
   a. He came to work late.
   b. He stayed at a friend's house.
   c. He got up too early.

2. Whose pants are these?
   a. They're blue.
   b. They're mine.
   c. They're at the tailor's.

3. Mary refuses to eat her vegetables.
   a. She chooses to eat them.
   b. She eats them all the time.
   c. She won't eat them.

4. Jack was almost electrocuted.
   a. Now he's a senator.
   b. Now he's in the hospital.
   c. Now he's an electrician.

5. He really means it.
   a. He's really mean.
   b. He isn't kidding.
   c. He really hates it.

6. David got into an argument with his sister.
   a. Did he get out of it?
   b. I'm happy to hear that.
   c. Is she still mad at him?

7. I didn't know whether . . .
   a. I should buy a dog or a cat.
   b. I must have bought a cat.
   c. could be so foggy in London.

8. If you go by the box office, please . . .
   a. pick up some boxes.
   b. pick up my tickets.
   c. put these in the mailbox.

9. My sister fell through the ice.
   a. She was skating and the pond was completely frozen.
   b. She was skating and the pond wasn't completely frozen.
   c. She was skating and eating ice cream.

10. The basketball game was so . . .
    a. enthusiastic.
    b. excited.
    c. exciting.

11. Walter got up on the wrong side of the bed.
    a. He's in a bad mood.
    b. He didn't make his bed.
    c. He didn't sleep on the right side.

12. You don't write legibly enough.
    a. You don't write often enough.
    b. Your letters are boring.
    c. I can't read your letters.

13. I'm a little concerned about Bill.
    a. He's been promoted.
    b. He's in a good mood.
    c. He's having trouble with his back.

14. I owe you an apology.
    a. I'll pay you back tomorrow.
    b. How much did it cost?
    c. I shouldn't have shouted so loudly.

15. I had a bad dream while . . .
    a. I was sleeping.
    b. I was eating in a restaurant.
    c. I was skiing.

16. I was born after my sister.
    a. She's older.
    b. I was chasing her.
    c. I wasn't very interested, and neither was she.

17. My friend Greta is a stewardess.
    a. Whenever there's anything wrong in our apartment building, she fixes it.
    b. She flies to interesting places all the time.
    c. Her recipe for stew is out of this world.

18. My grandfather likes to work out.
    a. He exercises often.
    b. He has a wonderful job.
    c. He's retired now.

▭ I. LISTEN

Listen to each word and then say it.

1. fill – feel
2. filling – feeling
3. fit – feed
4. his – he's

5. it – eat
6. knit – need
7. live – leave
8. living – leaving
9. rich – reach

10. still – steal
11. this – these
12. wig – week
13. will – we'll

▭ J. HAVE YOU HEARD?

Listen and complete the sentences.

fill	feel

1. a. . . . today?
   b. . . . out this income tax form?

still	steal

2. a. . . . cars?
   b. . . . take piano lessons?

this	these

3. a. . . . ice skates?
   b. . . . tennis racket?

knit	need

4. a. . . . very well.
   b. . . . anything at the store.

(continued) 43

live	leave

5. a. ... the party.

   b. ... in an apartment.

living	leaving

6. a. ... on the third floor.

   b. ... on the 6:00 plane.

his	he's

7. a. ... tired.

   b. ... alarm clock is broken.

it	eat

8. a. ... some potatoes instead.

   b. ... wasn't very fresh.

fit	feed

9. a. ... me.   They're just the right size.

   b. ... Rover.   They've just opened the can of dog food.

will	we'll

10. a. ... you be going on vacation, too?

    b. ... be flying to Madrid.

this	these

11. a. ... math problems.

    b. ... homework assignment.

wig	week

12. a. ... we're going to be very busy.

    b. ... needs a shampoo.

living	leaving

13. a. ... in Toronto.

    b. ... early.

rich	reach

14. a. ... Boston?

    b. ... and famous?

still	steal

15. a. ... anymore.

    b. ... go to high school.

fill	feel

16. a. ... a lot better in a few days.

    b. ... it out right away.

fit	feed

17. a. ... me enough.   I'm always hungry.

    b. ... me very well.   They're the wrong size.

his	he's

18. a. ... getting married.

    b. ... test was canceled.

rich	reach

19. a. ... New York.

    b. ... and successful.

it	eat

20. a. ... was my favorite recipe.

    b. ... a little more.

will	we'll

21. a. ... you be able to help us?

    b. ... have to call the TV repairman.

live	leave

22. a. ... in your neighborhood.

    b. ... at 5:00.

CHECK-UP TEST: *Chapters 3–4*

A. Complete the questions.

Ex. (What time does the concert begin?)

Could you please tell me _____ *what time the concert begins?* _____

1. (When will the next bus be leaving?)

Can you tell me _____

2. (Was Nancy in school yesterday?)

Do you know _____

3. (How much does this watch cost?)

Could you please tell me _____

4. (Is there a supermarket nearby?)

Could you tell me _____

5. (Why did Doris get up so early?)

Do you know _____

6. (Did Roger take his medicine this morning?)

Do you know _____

7. (How long have we been waiting?)

Do you have any idea _____

B. Complete the sentences

could have	might have	must have	should have	shouldn't have

(give)   *Ex.*   You ____*shouldn't*____ ____*have*____ ____*given*____ Mary eggs for
breakfast. She's allergic to them.

(practice)   1.   Gloria has won every chess game she's played today. She _____ _____

_____ a lot.

(do)   2.   I don't have anything to wear today. I _____ _____

_____ the laundry.

(vote)   3.   The people in our town _____ _____ _____
for anyone they wanted to. I don't understand why they voted for Peter Smith.

(drop)   4.   Jack lost his homework.   He _____ _____ _____ it on the way to school, or he _____ _____ _____ it on the bus.   He isn't sure what happened.

(study)   5.   You did very well on your test.   You _____ _____ _____ a lot.

(build)   6.   The Acme Company _____ _____ _____ their new office anywhere.   It was a mistake to build it here.

(wear)   7.   It's hot in here.   I _____ _____ _____ a heavy sweater today.

(feed)   8.   You _____ _____ _____ Rover.   He's been hungry all evening.

(fall)   9.   Lucy shouldn't have stood on that broken chair.   She _____ _____ _____ .

(buy)   10.   I _____ _____ _____ a used car.   My new car was much too expensive.

(spend)   11.   I _____ _____ _____ ten dollars, or I _____ _____ _____ twelve dollars.   I'm afraid I can't remember.

(go)   12.   You _____ _____ _____ swimming in the
(drown)   ocean yesterday.   It's very dangerous, and you _____ _____ _____ .

C. Listen and complete the sentences.

Ex. I don't know _____ *where your keys are* _____ .

1. I can't remember _____ .

2. I don't know _____ .

3. I have no idea _____ .

4. I don't know _____ .

5. I've forgotten _____ .

6. I don't know _____ .

A. YOU DECIDE: *If*

5

1. If I'm in a good mood, ...

2. .... if I'm in a bad mood.

3. If ...., he'll complain to his landlord.

4. If they don't stop making noise, ...

5. If ...., we'll have a party.

6. I'll have a nightmare if ....

7. If I can afford it, ...

8. You'll catch a bad cold if ....

9. We'll be very disappointed if ....

10. If I'm invited to the White House, ...

11. They'll wind up in jail if ....

12. If ...., you won't regret it.

13. You'll regret it if ....

B. LISTEN

Listen and complete the sentences.

1. a. ... I go to a movie.
    b. ... I'll go to a concert.

2. a. ... I'm hungry.
    b. ... I'll eat at a restaurant.

3. a. ... we miss the bus.
    b. ... we'll miss the train.

4. a. ... they go dancing.
    b. ... they'll go bowling.

5. a. ... we're late for school.
    b. ... we'll have to walk to work.

6. a. ... you miss the test.
    b. ... you'll miss the exam.

7. a. ... she doesn't study.
    b. ... she won't work harder.

8. a. ... he complains to his boss.
    b. ... he'll quit his job.

9. a. ... I decide to go skating.
    b. ... I'll decide to go sailing.

10. a. ... she has time.
    b. ... she won't be too busy.

11. a. ... I take them to the doctor.
    b. ... I'll call the nurse.

12. a. ... we have too much work.
    b. ... we'll be too busy.

C. YOU DECIDE: *What Might Happen?*

```
if _____ might _____
```

1. Miss Schultz, I really enjoy playing the piano. I'm going to practice EVERY DAY.

   That's wonderful. If _____ *you practice* _____

   every day, ... *you might* ....

   .... someday.

2. It's the boss's birthday. Why don't we send her flowers?

   That's a good idea. If _____

   her flowers, ...

   ....

3. Don't stay away too long. If _____

   too long, ...

   ....

4. I don't think little Jimmy should go skiing this

   weekend. It's MUCH too dangerous. It _____

   skiing this weekend, ...

   ....

5. You really should pay attention. If _____

   attention, ...

   ....

6.

You've known each other for only a few weeks. I really don't think you should get married so soon.   If _____ so soon,

. . . .

. . . .

7.

I don't want you to go hiking by yourself next weekend.

Why not?

It isn't a good idea.   If _____

by yourself, ...

. . . .

8.

Do you think I should work at Dad's hardware store when I finish college?

. . . .   If _____ at your

father's hardware store, ...

. . . .

D. YOU DECIDE: *What Should They Do?*

| if _____ might _____ |

1.

I don't think I'll ever get over this terrible cold.

Why don't you . . . . ?

If _____,

you might get over   your cold a little faster.

2.

Do you think Tommy will EVER stop crying?

I don't know.   Maybe we should . . . .

. . . .

If we _____,

_____ crying in a

little while.

(continued)   49

3.

I'm really confused. I'll never finish filling out this income tax form.

Why don't you ....? If _____, _____ sooner than you think.

4.

I can't fall asleep.

Maybe you should .... If _____, _____ more easily.

5.

I feel terribly depressed.

I think you should .... If _____ _____, _____ a lot better.

6.

My girlfriend and I had a terrible argument. She won't go out with me anymore.

Why don't you ....? If _____, _____ with you again.

7.

I need some advice. Every time I try to make chocolate chip cookies, they're terrible.

I'm sure they're just fine. But why don't you ....? If _____, _____ even better.

E. TOMORROW'S BASEBALL GAME

All the players on the Greenville Braves are talking about tomorrow's important baseball game.

1. We've won every game this year.

   I know. Isn't it wonderful?
   I hope _____*we win*_____ again tomorrow.

   If _____ tomorrow's game, we'll be the city champions.

2. Do you think it'll rain tomorrow?

   I hope not. If _____ tomorrow, our game will be canceled.

   And if tomorrow's game _____, everybody on the team

   _____ VERY disappointed. We've been looking forward to this

   game for a long time. I REALLY hope _____ rain.

3. That was a very fast ball you just caught. If you _____
   as well tomorrow, our team will probably win.

4. What happened, Jack? You missed a lot of balls in the last game.

   I know. But I'll try harder tomorrow.

   If _____ harder, I _____ as many balls.

   I hope you're right.

5. Would you like to go to a restaurant tonight?

   I really shouldn't. If _____ to a restaurant tonight, I'll

   eat too much. And if _____ too much, I won't be able to
   play well tomorrow. Let's go to a restaurant after the game.

6. Our car didn't start this morning. I sure

   hope _____ tomorrow. If it

   _____ tomorrow, I'll be late for the game. And if

   _____ for the game, the coach _____ very angry.

7.

I just spoke to Ellen.   She doesn't feel well at all.

I hope _____ better tomorrow.   If she

_____ better tomorrow, she won't be able to play.   And

if _____ in tomorrow's game, we'll probably lose.
How can one of our best players be sick at an important time like this?!

8.

Don't stay up too late tonight, Jim!

If _____ too late, you won't get a good night's sleep.

And if _____ enough sleep, you'll be too tired
to play well.

9.

I hope my mother _____ forget to bring the oranges

to the game.   If _____
to bring the oranges, we'll all be VERY hot and thirsty.

10.

I'm so nervous.   I hope _____ as nervous during
the game tomorrow.

You worry too much.   Losing isn't so terrible.

If _____ tomorrow's game, there will still be
a lot of other games.

11.

You've been playing very well this year, Paul.   I've invited
the coach of the Centerville Cubs to come to tomorrow's game.

If he _____ to tomorrow's game, and if you _____
very well, he'll probably offer you a contract with his team someday.

Do you REALLY think so?
If the coach of the Centerville Cubs _____ me
a contract, I'll be the happiest person in the world!

Good luck!

F. YOU DECIDE WHY

1.

Mr. Green, your daughter Sally doesn't get good grades in English because

she doesn't . . . . *do her homework carefully* . . . . ,

she doesn't . . . . ,

she doesn't . . . . ,

and she doesn't . . . .

If she _____ *did her homework carefully* _____ ,

if she _____ ,

if she _____ ,

and if she _____ ,

_____ much better grades. She's really a smart little girl.

2.

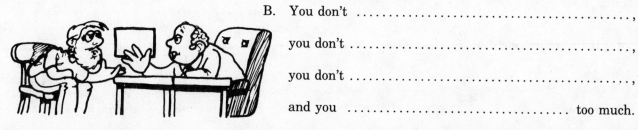

A. What's wrong with me, Doctor? Why don't I feel energetic anymore? I'm only thirty years old, and I feel tired all the time.

B. You don't . . . . ,

you don't . . . . ,

you don't . . . . ,

and you . . . . too much.

If you _____ ,

if you _____ ,

if you _____ ,

and if you _____ less,

_____ much more energetic.

(continued)   53

3.

A. How do you like your new job?

B. It's better than my old one, but I don't like it very much.

A. Really? Why not?

B. I don't .... ,

I'm not .... ,

my boss isn't .... ,

and the other employees don't ....

If _____ ,

if _____ ,

if _____ ,

and if _____ ,

_____ my job a lot more. I guess all jobs have their problems.

G. YOU DECIDE: *What Would You Do If?*

1. If I won a million dollars, ...

....

2. If I were an English teacher, ...

....

3. If I could travel anywhere in the world, ...

....

4. If I were president of ....

....

5. If I were .... years old again, ...

....

6. If I could have any job I wanted, ...

....

7. If today were the last day of my life, ...

....

H. YOU DECIDE: *What Must They Be Saying?*

1. I haven't had anything to eat all day.

   You must . . . . *be very hungry* . . . .

2. You've been driving for the past six hours.

   You must . . . .

3. Sheila didn't get the job she wanted.

   That's too bad.   She must . . . .

4. Ted went out with Jane on Monday, with Mary on Tuesday, with Louise on Wednesday, and with Sarah on Thursday.

   He must really . . . .

5. Lois hasn't been complaining about school recently.

   That's great.   She must . . . .

6. I'm going to be in the school play tomorrow.

   Really?   You must . . . .

7. Our neighbors spend all their weekends in the country.   Last weekend they went skiing, and this weekend they're going hiking.

   They must really . . . .

8. My son got the highest grades in his class.

   He must . . . .

   and you must . . . .

9. My husband has been watching the football game on TV all day, and there's an important baseball game he's going to watch all day tomorrow.

   He must really . . . . ,

   and you must . . . .

I. IF

1.

Paul really wants to get a raise.

If _____*he didn't want to get a raise*_____,

he _____*wouldn't work overtime*_____ every night.

2.

Timmy is afraid of the dark.

If _____*he weren't afraid of the dark*_____,

he _____*wouldn't be hiding under the bed*_____ right now.

3.

Nancy and Julie want to win the Boston Marathon.

If _____

_____ every day before and

after work.

4.

Michael's father is president of the company.

If his father _____,

Michael certainly _____ at
his boss right now.

5.

Peter wants to be just like his big brother.

If _____,

_____ every

weekend.

6.

My parents are away this afternoon.

If _____ _____,

_____ all

the ice cream in the refrigerator right now.

7. I hate being the oldest child in my family.

If _____,

I _____ have to _____

_____ all the time.

8. There's a police car in front of us.

If _____,

I _____
so slowly right now.

J. YOU DECIDE: *Why Doesn't Mary Like Her Neighborhood?*

Mary doesn't like her neighborhood because

....,

....,

....,

and ....

If _____,

if _____,

if _____,

and if _____,

_____ her neighborhood a lot more.

K. LISTEN

Listen to each word and then say it.

m!

1. might
2. maybe
3. mushroom
4. summer
5. someday
6. computer
7. remember
8. poems
9. warm
10. becoming

n!

1. night
2. never
3. noon
4. sunny
5. Sunday
6. confuse
7. explained
8. phones
9. worn
10. nice

L. _ARVI_'S BROKE_ TYPEWRITER

Marvin's typewriter is broken.   The m's and the n's don't always work.   Fill in the missing m's and n's and then read Marvin's letters aloud.

1.

Dear __a__cy,

   I really e__joyed visiti__g you i__ your __ew apart__e__t.
It's o__e of the __icest apart__e__ts I've ever see__. I liked
everythi__g about it: the __oder__ kitche__ a__d bathroo__s,
the elega__t livi__g roo__ and di__i__g roo__, a__d the
su__y bedroo__s. I ca__'t believe there's eve__ a garde__ i__
fro__t of the buildi__g with le__o__s a__d ora__ges.
   I thi__k you'll be very happy i__ your __ew __eighborhood.
It's certai__ly very co__ve__ie__t to be so __ear a super__arket,
a __ovie theater, a__d a trai__ statio__.
   I'__ looki__g forward to seei__g you agai__ a__d __eeting
your __ew __eighbors.

                                   __arvi__

2.

To Who_ It _ay Co_cer_:

I reco_ _e_d Joh_ A_derso_ for the job of head _echanic at Ji_'s Gas Station. During the _i_e years I've k_ow_ hi_, he's bee_ a_ excelle_t e_ployee a_d a ki_d and ho_est frie_d. He's _ever _issed a day's work at our co_pany, and he's always bee_ o_ ti_e. But _ost i_porta_t of all, Joh_ A_derso_ really u_dersta_ds what _akes a car ru_.

Si_cerely,
_r. _arvi_ _elso_
_a_ager

3.

Dear _orma_,

I just fi_ished reading your _ost rece_t poe_s, a_d i_ _y opi_io_, they're _ag_ificent. The poe_ about the opti_istic co_puter is very a_using, but _y favorite o_es are "The Moo_ and the _ou_tai_" a_d "U_der _y U_brella." They're fa_tastic!

According to _y wife, _ildred, you're beco_ing fa_ous in _any foreig_ cou_tries, and your poe_s are bei_g tra_slated i_to Russia_, Fre_ch, Ger_a_, Italia_, Spa_ish, and Japa_ese. I thi_k that's wo_derful.

Have you begu_ writi_g your _ext _ew _ovel yet? I wo_der whe_ we'll be hearing _ore about it.

arvi

4.

Dear To_,

Re_e_ber whe_ you explai_ed to _e how to _ake your _other's fa_ous Italia_ chicke_ a_d wi_e with _ushroo_s? Well, I _ade so_e for di__er last _ight, and I'_ afraid so_ethi_g _ust have go_e wro_g. I _ight have put i_ too _a_y to_atoes, or _aybe I did_'t put i_ e_ough o_io_s a_d _ushroo_s. I do_'t k_ow what happe_ed, but I k_ow I _ust have _ade so_e _istakes because _obody e_joyed it very _uch. _ildred and Ja_e did_'t co_plai_, but they said yours was _uch _ore delicious than _ine.

Do you thi_k you could se_d your _other's recipe so_eti_e soo_ so I ca_ try it agai_? Whe_ you explai_ed it to _e, I should have writte_ it dow_.

arvi

A. TIMOTHY'S EXCUSES

Timothy never wants to do ANYTHING or go ANYWHERE.
Whenever someone asks him, he always has an excuse.

1. Timothy, would you like to go skating this weekend?

I'm sorry, but I don't have any skates.

If _____I had_____ a pair of skates, __I'd__ love to go.

2. Would you like to go jogging with us?

Thank you for asking, but I don't run as fast as you and your friends. If _____ a little faster, _____ happy to go.

3. Professor Michaels is giving a lecture on modern poetry tomorrow. Why don't we go together?

Unfortunately, I don't understand modern poetry at all. If _____ it just a little, _____ very glad to go.

4. Your favorite movie is at the Main Street Theater. Would you like to see it again?

7:00.

Maybe. What time does it begin?

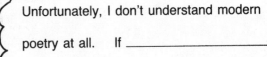

That's very early. If _____ _____ a little later, _____ happy to go.

5. Would you like to go bowling?

I'm sorry, but I don't feel very well.

If _____ a little better,

_____ very happy to go.

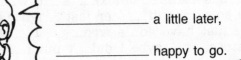

60

6. Your father doesn't need the car tonight. We can go to the baseball game on the other side of town.

Unfortunately, I never drive at night.

If _____ at night, _____ _____ glad to take you to the baseball game.

7. Let's go to a night club!

I don't know how to dance. If _____ _____, _____ love to go to a night club.

8. We're spending a few days at my uncle's summer house. We'd love you to come.

I'm afraid I don't sleep very well at other people's houses. If _____ better at other people's houses, _____ _____ glad to go.

9. Everybody in our class is going to be in the school play. How about you?

I'm afraid I can't. I don't sing or dance or act well enough, and I speak much too softly.

If _____ or _____ or _____ better, and if _____ louder, _____ in the play, too.

10. Would you like to . . . .
. . . .
. . . . ?

Unfortunately, I don't . . . .
. . . .
If . . . .
. . . .
. . . .

B. YOU DECIDE: *If*

1.

Do you think Mom would be happy if I . . . .
. . . . ?

Of course _____*she would*_____.   _____*She'd be*_____ very happy.   That's a wonderful idea.

2.

Do you think Dad would be upset if I . . . .
. . . . ?

I'm sure _____.   _____ very upset.   That's a terrible idea.

3.

Do you think the boss would be angry if I . . . .
. . . . ?

I'm afraid _____.   _____ very angry.

4.

Do you think our grandchildren would be happy if we . . . .
. . . . ?

Of course _____.   _____ very happy.   I'm glad you thought of it.

5.

Do you think our teacher would be annoyed if . . . .
. . . . ?

You know _____.   _____ very annoyed.

6.

Do you think my wife would be upset if . . . .
. . . . ?

Of course _____.   _____ very upset.

62

C. YOU DECIDE: *What Does Herbert Wish?*

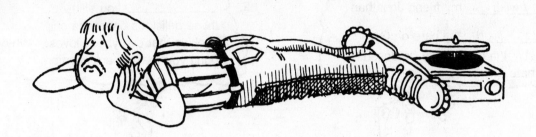

My friend Herbert isn't very happy.   He's never satisfied with anything.

1. He lives in Greenville.

   He wishes . . . .

2. His father is a salesman.

   Herbert wishes . . . .

3. His mother teaches English at his school.

   He wishes . . . .

4. Herbert has three older sisters.

   He wishes . . . .

5. His father drives an old used car.

   He wishes . . . .

6. At school Herbert studies math and science.

   He wishes . . . .

7. Herbert speaks French fluently, but he doesn't know anybody else who can speak it.

   He wishes . . . .

8. He also takes clarinet lessons.

   He wishes . . . .

9. After school, he works in a library.

   He wishes . . . .

10. Herbert also . . . .

   He wishes . . . .

D. I WISH

1. _____I wish_____ my friend Jonathan still _____lived_____ here on Green Street. I'm really sorry he doesn't live here anymore.

2. _____ you still _____ those delicious chocolate chip cookies that everybody loves. Why don't you make them anymore?

3. _____ they still _____ our favorite desserts at this store. It's too bad they stopped selling them.

4. _____ Rita still _____ _____. It's a shame she doesn't take them anymore. She always enjoyed her karate lessons when she was in the class.

5. _____ better today. I really don't feel well at all.

6. _____ as well as my brother does. He has a very beautiful voice.

7. _____ poetry. Teaching poetry is much more interesting than teaching grammar.

8. _____ my son and daughter _____ along better. They'd be much happier if they didn't argue so much.

9. _____ _____. Dogs are the best pets in the world.

10. _____ it _____. When it's 5:00, I can leave work.

64

E. LOOKING FOR A JOB

Employment Agency

A. I wonder if you can help me. I'm looking for a job as a French teacher.

B. Most of our schools want their French teachers to teach more than one language. Can you teach Spanish or German?

A. I wish ____*I could*____, but my Spanish and German aren't good enough.
   1

B. That's too bad. If _____ speak Spanish or German, _____ able to
   2   3
   find a job easily. Hmm. The Flower School is looking for someone to teach French and music.
   They want someone who knows a lot about music and can play the piano and sing.

A. I know a lot about music and I have a very good voice, but I can't play the piano.

B. What a shame! If _____, the Flower
   4
   School _____ VERY interested in you.
            5

A. And the Flower School is one of the best schools in town. I wish _____
                                                                        6
   play the piano.

B. Well, the Park School is also a very fine school, and they're looking for someone to teach French

   and .... They want someone who knows a lot about ....
        7   8
   and can ....
                                                                                          9

A. I'm afraid I can't _____.
                      10

B. That's too bad. If _____, the
                       11
   Park School _____ interested in you. Maybe you should think about finding
                12
   an office job. How fast can you type?

A. Forty words a minute.

B. I wish you _____ a little faster. If _____ 60 words a
              13   14
   minute, _____ any trouble finding a job. Wait a minute!
            15
   Here's a job you might like. The Reliable Insurance Company is looking for a salesperson who
   can travel all over the country.

A. I wish _____, but I have two small children at home.
           16

B. There must be a lot of other things you can do. Can you ....

   ....?
                                                                                              17

(continued)

A. Not really.

B. That's too bad, because if _____

_____18

_____ send you for an interview with the .... Company. I'm
____19   ____20

terribly sorry, but those are all the jobs I have today. I wish _____ help you. Come
                                                                        21

back in a week. Maybe I'll be able to find you something then.

A. Thank you.

F. YOU DECIDE WHY

1.

A. I'm really annoyed with the boss because

   he always .... *gives us a lot of work* ....

   he always ....

   and he's ....

B. You're right.

   I wish he _____ *didn't give us a lot of work* _____

   I wish _____

   And I wish _____
   Unfortunately, there's nothing we can do about it.

2.

A. I hate it when your Aunt Gertrude comes to visit.

   She always ....

   she always ....

   and she's ....

B. I know.

   I wish _____

   I wish _____

   And I wish _____
   But she's my aunt, and I can't tell her to leave.

G. WHAT DOES IT MEAN?

Put a circle around the appropriate answer.

1. I'm positive we're having a test tomorrow.
   a. I'm afraid we might have a test.
   b. I think we'll probably have a test.
   c. I'm sure we're having a test.

2. Our teacher is never annoyed.
   a. She never enjoys anything.
   b. She's never in a good mood.
   c. She's never upset.

3. Albert dropped out of school.
   a. He skipped a few classes.
   b. He quit school.
   c. He ran home from school as quickly as he could.

4. Mrs. Jones wants to teach something else.
   a. She wants to teach the same thing again.
   b. She wants to teach at a different time.
   c. She wants to teach a different subject.

5. We're going to give Janet a telescope because
   a. she always calls up her friends.
   b. she's interested in chemistry.
   c. she's interested in astronomy.

6. I wish Edward were more aggressive.
   a. Edward is too shy.
   b. Edward gets into too many arguments.
   c. Edward should try to be more polite.

7. Ever since I heard that we're having an important exam next week, I've been concentrating on my work a lot more.
   a. I've been complaining more about my work.
   b. I've been paying more attention to my work.
   c. I've been worrying more.

8. We live in a high-rise building.
   a. Our apartment building isn't very large, but the rents are high.
   b. Our house is in the mountains.
   c. Our building has many floors.

9. My birthday was last Friday. I'm celebrating it today.
   a. I'm thinking about my birthday today.
   b. I'm having a birthday party today.
   c. I'm taking down the party decorations today.

10. I had trouble answering the questions.
    a. The questions were confusing.
    b. The questions were amusing.
    c. I answered all the questions three times.

11. You'll get better grades if
    a. you go hiking in the mountains.
    b. you go shopping at a better store.
    c. you study harder.

12. Jack is satisfied with his new job.
    a. He can't stand his new job.
    b. He likes his new job.
    c. His new job makes him very tired.

13. William really enjoys nature.
    a. He enjoys going to concerts.
    b. He enjoys going to museums.
    c. He enjoys taking long walks in the country.

14. Fred and Louise don't have enough in common.
    a. They don't get paid enough.
    b. They aren't interested in the same things.
    c. They don't have enough clothes.

15. Michael always tells the truth.
    a. You can always believe Michael.
    b. Michael should be more honest.
    c. Michael tells interesting stories.

16. Inflation is getting worse.
    a. Everything costs less.
    b. Prices are getting higher.
    c. Everything used to be more expensive.

17. Mr. Rogers sells books.
    a. He's a salesman.
    b. He's a librarian.
    c. He's a translator.

H. SOUND IT OUT

Listen to each word and then say it.

fell:		fail:	
1.	eggs	1.	ate
2.	special	2.	space
3.	athletic	3.	operation
4.	bread	4.	break
5.	pleasure	5.	plays
6.	many	6.	main

Listen and put a circle around the word that has the same sound.

1.	bed:	grade	get	stayed
2.	late:	take	test	terrible
3.	ready:	reach	great	Ted
4.	parade:	pet	paid	pepper
5.	face:	rest	vacation	less
6.	Fred:	Edward	Frieda	afraid
7.	complain:	then	said	Spain
8.	weigh:	they'll	tell	jealous
9.	spent:	sprain	Jane	when

Now make a sentence using all the words you circled. Read the sentence aloud.

10. _____ _____ and _____ _____ _____, _____ _____

a _____ in _____.

11.	toothpaste:	best	play	past
12.	hate:	hat	eight	head
13.	chemistry:	tennis	came	cat
14.	lesson:	late	great	let's
15.	upset:	skate	made	next
16.	wait:	wealthy	Jane	instead
17.	mend:	mail	Wednesday	plane
18.	friend:	Fred	wait	same

Now make a sentence using all the words you circled. Read the sentence aloud.

19. _____ _____ _____ with _____ and _____ _____

_____ at _____ o'clock.

A. YOU DECIDE WHY

1. A. Why didn't you enjoy your vacation?

   B. It's a long story. The weather wasn't .... *warm enough* ....,

      I didn't bring ....,

      I wasn't able to ....,

      the hotel didn't have ....,

      .... weren't ....,

      and .... didn't write to me while I was away.

   A. What a shame!

   B. Yes, I was very frustrated. If the weather _____ *had been warm enough* _____,

      if I _____,

      if I _____,

      if the hotel _____,

      if _____,

      and if _____ while I was away,

      I know _____ *I would have enjoyed* _____ my vacation.

2. A. Why didn't you go to the symphony with us last weekend? You missed a wonderful concert.

   B. I was planning to go, but I didn't ....,

      I wasn't ....,

      and .... didn't ....

      If I _____,

      if I _____,

      and if _____,

      I _____ to the symphony with you.

   A. Well, maybe we can go again next week.

3. A. I wonder why I wasn't hired by the Century Insurance Company. Do you think it's because at the job interview

I didn't ....,

I didn't ....,

I didn't ....,

and I wasn't ....?

B. I'm sure that's why.

If _____,

if _____,

if _____,

and if _____,

I'm positive you _____ by the Century Insurance Company. I hope you don't make the same mistakes at your next job interview.

4. A. Why didn't you eat your dinner? I spent ALL afternoon cooking for you.

B. I didn't ....,

I wasn't ....,

.... wasn't ....,

and .... weren't ....,

If I _____,

if I _____,

if _____,

and if _____,

I _____ my dinner.

B. YOU DECIDE: *What Should They Have Done?*

A. I'm afraid your grandparents didn't have a very good time when they visited us last weekend.

B. I know, and I feel terrible about it. They didn't eat anything we served them, and they were very bored and uncomfortable in our apartment.

We should have ....,

we should have ....,

and we should have ....

If we _____,

if _____,

and if _____,

I'm sure my grandparents _____ a much better time.

C. HOW I BECAME A MUSICIAN

A. Why did you decide to become a musician?

B. When I was very young, my parents took me to concerts every weekend, my grandparents bought me a violin, and my mother gave me violin lessons. When I was older, I studied music in high school and college, and I sang in the school choir.

If my parents _____*hadn't taken me to concerts*_____ every weekend,
1

if my grandparents _____,
2

if my mother _____,
3

if I _____ in high school and college,
4

and if I _____,
5

I _____*wouldn't have become*_____ a musician.
6

71

D. YOU DECIDE: *Why Was Jim Late for Work?*

I'm really sorry I was so late for work this morning. I tried to get here on time, but EVERYTHING went wrong.

First, ...

Then, ...

After that, ...

And also, ...

If _____,

if _____,

if _____,

and if _____,

I _____ so late.

E. YOU DECIDE: *How Did Everybody Help?*

This is the most exciting day of the year in Hollywood. It's the day the best actors, actresses, and movie directors receive rewards for the movies they have made. Hundreds of movie stars and movie makers have been invited to the awards ceremony. They're sitting nervously in the audience. In a few minutes, they'll know who has been chosen best director of the year.

And the best director of the year is Roger Vanderbilt!

I want to thank everybody who voted for me for this award.   But I couldn't have made this movie by myself.   Many people helped.

.... wrote the exciting story.

.... designed the elegant costumes.

.... and .... acted magnificently.

Also, my wife ....,

and my children ....

If _____,

if _____,

if _____,

and also if my wife _____,

and if my children _____,
I never would have been able to make this movie.

F.   I'M REALLY GLAD

I'm really glad I went to the Gold Star Business School.

If ___*I hadn't gone*___ to the Gold Star Business School, I ___*wouldn't have*___
      1   2
learned to program a computer.

And if I _____ a computer,
                                                                                        3

I _____ a job at the Reliable Insurance Company.
                                                    4

And if I _____ a job at the Reliable Insurance Company,
                                        5

I _____ to Los Angeles on business.
                                                          6

And if I _____ to Los Angeles on business, I _____
                                        7

_____ met your mother.
                    8

And if _____, you _____ born!
                                    9   10

73

G. WHY DIDN'T YOU TELL ME?

1. Why didn't you tell me your parents were coming to dinner?

   If you _____ 1 me your parents were coming to dinner, I would have _____ 2 some more food.

   And if _____ 3 some more food, there would have been enough for everybody to eat.

   And if _____ 4 for everybody to eat, we _____ _____ 5 to an expensive restaurant.

   And if we _____ 6 to an expensive restaurant, we _____ 7 so much money!

2. Why didn't you tell me our English class was canceled?

   If _____ 1 our English class was canceled, I _____ 2 to school yesterday afternoon.

   And if _____ 3 to school yesterday afternoon, I _____ _____ 4 at home when the TV repairman came to pick up the TV.

   And if I _____ 5 at home when the TV repairman came to pick up the TV, he _____ 6 able to take it to his repair shop.

   And if the TV repairman _____ 7 able to take the TV to his repair shop, I'm sure he _____ 8 fixed it.

   And if the TV repairman _____ 9 the TV, we'd be watching it right now!

H. THE COMPANY PICNIC

1. Did you go to the company picnic last Saturday?

   Yes, I did, and it was terrible.   I wish I ____*hadn't*____ ____*gone*____.
   There were a lot of things I could have done that day.   I wish I

   _____ _____ something else.

2. I wish more people from our department _____ _____ at

   the picnic.   I didn't know very many people at all.   If I _____

   _____ more people at the picnic last Saturday, I _____

   _____ _____ so lonely and I _____

   _____ so *out of place*.

3. Why weren't the employees from the Greenville office invited to the picnic?   I

   expected them to be there.   If they _____ _____ invited to the

   picnic, it _____ _____ _____ much livelier.

4. I wish I _____ forget people's names all the time.   Can you believe it?
   At the picnic last Saturday, I couldn't remember Harry's wife's name, and

   I had met her a dozen times before.   I wish I hadn't _____

   her name.   After all, if she _____ forgotten MY name, I _____

   _____ liked it.

(continued)

5.

I know Jeffrey loves to cook, but I wish he _____ ALWAYS _____ at our company picnics.   And I CERTAINLY wish he _____ _____ at the picnic last Saturday!   If Jeffrey _____ _____ at the picnic last Saturday, he _____ _____ burned all the hamburgers, and we _____ _____ had to eat them.

You're right.   I wish I _____ _____ a big breakfast before I went to the picnic.   If I _____ _____ a big breakfast that morning, I _____ _____ _____ so hungry, and I _____ _____ _____ all those terrible hamburgers.

6.

Betty didn't bring her little son to the picnic because she was exhausted, and she didn't want to take care of him all afternoon.   She shouldn't have worried.   If Betty _____ _____ her little son to the picnic, I _____ _____ _____ care of him because I love children.   I wish Betty _____ _____ her son to the picnic.

7.

I know Brenda loves to sing and play the guitar, but I wish she _____ ALWAYS _____ and _____ the guitar at company picnics.

And I CERTAINLY wish she _____ _____ and _____ the guitar last Saturday!   She has the worst voice I've ever heard, and she plays the guitar VERY badly!   If Brenda _____ _____ and _____ the guitar at the picnic last Saturday, I _____ _____ _____ a headache all that evening.

8.

Aren't you glad that the weather was warm and sunny last Saturday?

No, not really.   To tell the truth, I wish _____ _____ rained.

If it _____ _____ last Saturday, the picnic _____ _____ _____ canceled, and I _____ _____ _____ able to stay home and read a good book.

9.

I wish I _____ _____ the potato salad at the picnic. It didn't taste very fresh.

You should have tried the bean salad. It was delicious!

Bean salad? By the time I got to the picnic, there wasn't any.

If there _____ _____ some bean salad at the picnic

when I arrived, I certainly _____ _____ had some.

10.

I was very bored at the picnic last Saturday.

That's because you just sat and talked all afternoon. You should have

. . . . or . . . .

If you _____,

or if you _____,

you _____ so bored.

I. HOPES AND WISHES

1. A. Can you go skating with us next weekend?

   B. I wish I _____*could go skating*_____ with you, but I'm afraid I'm busy.

   I hope we _____*can go skating*_____ another time.

2. A. Do you enjoy living in Centerville?

   B. Life in Centerville is very boring. I wish _____ someplace more exciting. Fortunately, my parents are looking for an apartment in Hollywood. I hope

   they _____ one soon.

3. A. I wish Mrs. Larson _____ us so much homework all the time.

   B. I usually don't mind having a lot of homework, but I hope we _____ much homework tomorrow because I'm going to be very busy.

4. A. I'm having trouble learning to swim. I'm afraid I'm too old. I wish _____

_____ to swim when I was younger.

B. Don't be ridiculous! You do a lot better than many of the younger students in our

swimming class. They all wish they _____ as well as you.

5. A. I wish somebody _____ the dog before we left the house this morning,
but there's nothing we can do about it now. Poor Rover must be very hungry. I hope

your sister _____ him when she gets home.

B. I'm sure she will.

6. A. I hope you _____ busy tomorrow. If you _____ too busy, we can see a
movie together.

B. I wish you _____ me sooner because I've already made other plans.
Why don't you ask me again some other time?

7. A. I wish you _____ have to leave. I'm really going to miss you. I hope you

_____ a good time while you're away, but don't enjoy yourself TOO MUCH.

B. I'm going to miss you, too. I wish you _____ going with me.

8.

I had my yearly checkup today, and my doctor is a little concerned about my weight.

He wishes I _____ so heavy. He gave me a new diet that I'm going to try.

I hope _____ a lot of weight.

J. YOU DECIDE: *If*

1. I hope my neighbors stop talking soon.   If they don't stop talking soon, ...
....
....

2. I wish I had more free time.   If I had more free time, ...
....
....

3. I hope my parents aren't in a bad mood today.   If they're in a bad mood, ...
....
....

4. I wish I didn't have to .... If I didn't have to
...., ...
....

5. I hope you can lend me .... If you can lend me
...., ...
....

6. I wish I had .... when I was younger.
If .... when I was younger,
....

7. I hope .... is elected President.   If ....
.... is elected President, ...
....

8. I wish I knew more about .... If I knew more
about ...., ...
....

Listen and complete the sentences.

1. a. . . . I won't be so lonely.
    b. . . . I wouldn't be so bored.

2. a. . . . I'll be home right away.
    b. . . . I wouldn't be late.

3. a. . . . he'd be a lot happier.
    b. . . . he'll have a lot more friends.

4. a. . . . I'd give her a telescope.
    b. . . . I'll teach her about computers.

5. a. . . . we'd have lunch together.
    b. . . . we'll finish the story we've been writing.

6. a. . . . I won't have to walk to work.
    b. . . . I wouldn't have to ride my bicycle to work.

 L. LISTEN: *Hopes and Wishes*

Listen and complete the sentences.

1. a. . . . he isn't sick.
    b. . . . he felt better.

2. a. . . . tomorrow's lesson is easier.
    b. . . . I understood English better.

3. a. . . . she visits me more often.
    b. . . . she still lived across the street.

4. a. . . . she worked someplace else.
    b. . . . she can find another job.

5. a. . . . I had learned when I was younger.
    b. . . . you can teach me how.

6. a. . . . I'm a more graceful dancer.
    b. . . . I weren't so clumsy.

7. a. . . . you can come.
    b. . . . you could be there.

8. a. . . . he were more careful.
    b. . . . he finds it soon.

9. a. . . . everybody likes apple pie.
    b. . . . it tasted good.

10. a. . . . she cooks better.
    b. . . . she had taken cooking lessons.

11. a. . . . you knew more about TVs.
    b. . . . you know how to fix it.

12. a. . . . she had bought a new car.
    b. . . . it starts on cold days.

13. a. . . . we had a few more.
    b. . . . we can borrow a few.

14. a. . . . I have a better memory.
    b. . . . I could remember it.

 M. LISTEN

Listen to each word and then say it.

1. f<u>e</u>ll – f<u>ai</u>l
2. ch<u>e</u>ck – sh<u>a</u>ke
3. Fr<u>e</u>d – afr<u>ai</u>d
4. m<u>e</u>n – M<u>ai</u>n
5. m<u>e</u>t – m<u>a</u>de

6. n<u>e</u>ver – n<u>ei</u>ghbor
7. p<u>e</u>pper – p<u>a</u>per
8. p<u>e</u>t – p<u>ai</u>d
9. t<u>e</u>ller – t<u>ai</u>lor
10. w<u>e</u>dding – w<u>ai</u>ting

80

N. HAVE YOU HEARD?

Listen and complete the sentences.

met	made

1. a. ... all the beds.
   b. ... an old friend.

fell	fail

2. a. ... when they went skating yesterday.
   b. ... whenever they take a test.

teller	tailor

3. a. ... works in a bank.
   b. ... takes in your clothes.

pepper	paper

4. a. ... in my notebook.
   b. ... in my soup.

Fred	afraid

5. a. ... Smith?
   b. ... you might drown?

met	made

6. a. ... any summer plans yet?
   b. ... their new neighbors?

men	Main

7. a. ... Street bus is leaving.
   b. ... are leaving the barber shop.

check	shake

8. a. ... hands.
   b. ... with the mechanic.

wedding	waiting

9. a. ... at the bus stop.
   b. ... was the happiest day of my life.

pepper	paper

10. a. ... on my hamburger.
    b. ... for my composition.

never	neighbor

11. a. ... just moved in yesterday.
    b. ... flown in an airplane before.

teller	tailor

12. a. ... at the bank.
    b. ... because I like to sew.

pet	paid

13. a. ... her income tax.
    b. ... bird knows how to talk.

check	shake

14. a. ... with the ticket agent.
    b. ... hands with the ticket agent.

fell	fail

15. a. ... most of my English exams.
    b. ... asleep very late last night.

pet	paid

16. a. ... the electric bill.
    b. ... dog barked all night.

wedding	waiting

17. a. ... is at 3:00.
    b. ... for us.

never	neighbor

18. a. ... sometimes borrows Roger's cassette player.
    b. ... been to Rome.

men	Main

19. a. ... Street subway station?
    b. ... who were working here?

Fred	afraid

20. a. ... I'll get hurt.
    b. ... Jones. What's your name?

CHECK-UP TEST: *Chapters 5–7*

A. Fill in the blanks.

1. Philip takes piano lessons, but he doesn't enjoy them. He wishes he _____ guitar lessons.

2. Jane studied French last year, and she hated it. She wishes she _____ _____ something else.

3. Richard doesn't enjoy being single. He wishes he _____ married.

4. Mrs. Smith drives an old used car. She wishes she _____ a more reliable car.

5. By the time John got to the party, most of his friends had already left. John wishes he _____ _____ to the party sooner.

6. My neighbor's son practices the violin every afternoon and every evening. I wish he _____ _____ the violin so often.

7. Mario doesn't speak English very well. He wishes he _____ more fluently.

8. You ate all the cookies in the cookie jar. I wish you _____ _____ them all.

B. Complete the sentences.

1. If we can afford it, _____ _____ on vacation next month.

2. I'll send you a letter if _____ _____ the time.

3. If Tom were more careful, _____ _____ a better driver.

4. If Susan didn't enjoy music, _____ _____ _____ to concerts every week.

5. If I had studied a little harder, _____ _____ _____ _____ well on yesterday's test.

6. If I _____ _____ a raise soon, I'll complain to my boss.

7. If Janet _____ more patient, she'd get along better with her brother.

8. If you stay up too late tonight, _____ _____ get a good night's sleep.

9. My parents _____ _____ disappointed if I fail this exam.

10. If you _____ the dog more often, he wouldn't be so hungry.

82

C. Complete the sentences.

1. Sidney doesn't have many friends because he isn't outgoing enough.

   If he _____ more outgoing, _____ _____ a lot of friends.

2. Alan feels tired all the time because he works too hard.

   If he _____ _____ so hard, _____ _____ _____ so tired all the time.

3. Rita didn't enjoy her vacation because the weather wasn't warm.

   If the weather _____ _____ warm, she _____ _____

   _____ her vacation.

4. Julia arrived very late because she missed the bus.

   If she _____ _____ the bus, she _____ _____

   _____ so late.

5. I'm very frustrated because I can't type fast enough.

   If I _____ _____ faster, _____ _____ _____ so frustrated.

6. Ivan made a lot of mistakes because he wasn't paying attention.

   If he _____ _____ _____ attention, he _____ _____

   _____ so many mistakes.

7. Doris looks very confused because she doesn't understand today's grammar.

   If she _____ today's grammar, she _____ _____ so confused.

D. Listen and complete the sentences.

Ex. (a) . . . she still lived at home.
  b. . . . she doesn't forget to write.

1. a. . . . she felt better.
   b. . . . she gets better soon.

2. a. . . . you were here.
   b. . . . it doesn't rain.

3. a. . . . we don't get lost.
   b. . . . I had written it down.

4. a. . . . I knew the answer.
   b. . . . I can figure it out.

5. a. . . . we lived in a bigger apartment.
   b. . . . we can move soon.

6. a. . . . it's easy.
   b. . . . he didn't have to take it.

7. a. . . . she doesn't get hurt.
   b. . . . she were a more careful skier.

8. a. . . . we get there on time.
   b. . . . it didn't start so early.

83

A. WHAT THE MAILMAN BROUGHT

> Dear Mother,
>   I just married my philosophy professor.

1. A. I got a letter from my daughter at Greenville College last week.

    B. Really?   What did she say?

    A. She said _____ *she had just married her philosophy professor* _____.

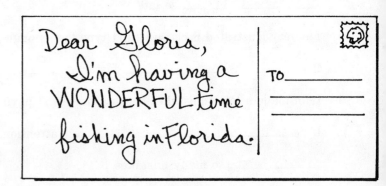

> Dear Gloria,
>   I'm having a WONDERFUL time fishing in Florida.
>
> TO _____

2. A. I got a postcard from my Aunt Betty last Saturday.

    B. Oh, that's nice.   What did she say?

    A. She said _____

    _____.

> Dear Professor Thompson,
>   I read about your new book in yesterday's newspaper.

3. A. I got a letter from one of my former students yesterday.

    B. Really?   What did he say?

    A. He said _____

    _____.

4. A. I heard from the Browns last week.

   B. You did? What did they say?

   A. They said _____

   _____

> DEAR MICHAEL,
>   WE HOPE YOU CAN VISIT US WHEN YOU COME TO CHICAGO ON YOUR NEXT BUSINESS TRIP.

> Dear Mr. Baker,
>   I'm very sorry, but you aren't the right person for the job.

5. A. I'm so depressed! I finally heard from the manager of the computer company where I had that job interview.

   B. Oh, no! What did he say?

   A. He told me _____

   _____

> Dear Mrs. Hanson,
>   I'm very busy and I can't begin repairing your roof until next month.

6. A. I've been trying to get my roof fixed for months, and yesterday I got ANOTHER letter from the carpenter.

   B. Not again! What did he say this time?

   A. He said _____

   _____

> Dear Brian,
>   I was hoping to send you some more money for college this year, but now I won't be able to because I'm having business problems.

7. A. I'm so worried. I got a letter from my father last week.

    B. What did he say?

    A. He told me _____

    _____ .

> Dear .... ,
>   You won't believe it, but ....
> ....
> ....
> ....

8. A. Did you hear that I got
        a letter from Kathy
        last Wednesday?

    B. No, I didn't. What did she say?

    A. She said _____

    _____ .

> Dear Mom,
>   I'll be arriving ....
> ....
> ....
> ....
>
> To _____
>   _____
>   _____

9. A. I'm so excited. I got a postcard from my son in the army.

    B. You did? What did he say?

    A. He said _____

    _____ .

Dear ....,
    I enjoyed ....
....
....
....

10. A. I got the nicest letter
       from my friend Louise.

    B. Really?   What did she say?

    A. She told me _____

       _____

Dear ....,
    Your nephew has been ....
....
....
....

11. A. I heard from my sister yesterday.   She's very concerned about her youngest son.

    B. Oh, dear!   What did she say about him?

    A. She said _____

       _____

Dear ....,
    I'm finally going to ....
....
....
....

12. A. I got a letter from
       Peter last week.
       I'm so happy for him!

    B. Why?   What did he say?

    A. He said _____

       _____

(continued)

Dear ....,
  I was promoted last month, and
....
....
....

13. A. I heard from Jennifer yesterday.   She's really doing well.

    B. That's good!   What did she say?

    A. She said _____

    _____

B. YOU DECIDE: *What Happened While Peter Williams Was Away?*

Peter Williams just returned home after studying in Europe for two years.

GEORGE: Welcome home, Peter!   I'm so glad you're back.   How have you been?

PETER: Just fine.   What's been happening since I've been away?

GEORGE: Well, your old girlfriend Julie got married last month.

PETER: She did?   I didn't know _____*she had gotten married last month*_____.
        1
        I wonder why she didn't write me.

GEORGE: She probably thought you knew.   Have you heard about Sam?   He's in the hospital.

PETER: Really?   I had no idea _____.
        2
        What happened?   Was it his heart?

GEORGE: Yes.   He had another heart attack last week.

88

PETER: That's terrible! I knew _____ having problems with his heart for the
3
past several years, but I didn't know _____ another heart attack. Tell me,
4
how's your brother Frank?

GEORGE: Haven't you heard? He's going to become president of his company next month.

PETER: That's wonderful! I knew he _____ promoted many times in the past
5
several years, but I didn't know _____

_____.
6

GEORGE: And you must have heard about Betty and Fred. They ....

....
7

PETER: Really? I didn't know _____

_____.
8
Tell me, how are your children?

GEORGE: Well, they've been having some problems. My son ....

....,
9
and my daughter ....

....
10

PETER: That's a shame! I didn't know your son _____

_____,
11
and your daughter _____

_____.
12

GEORGE: Well, it's been nice talking to you. Say hello to your roommate Ralph.

PETER: Oh, you probably didn't know. Ralph isn't living here anymore. He ....

....
13
and ....
14
I would have told you before, but I thought EVERYBODY knew that Ralph _____

_____
15
and _____

_____.
16

1. That's wonderful!   I didn't know _____ *he wanted to be a dentist* _____

   _____

2. Really?   I didn't know _____

   _____

3. Really?   I didn't know _____

   _____

4. Are you sure?   I didn't know _____

   _____

5. Really?   I didn't know _____

   _____

6. I don't believe it!   I didn't know _____

   _____

7. That's wonderful!   I didn't know _____

   _____

8. Really?   I didn't know _____

   _____

9. I'm sorry.   I didn't know _____

   _____

10. I can't believe it!   I didn't know _____

    _____

11. That's wonderful!   I didn't know _____

    _____

12. Really?   I didn't know _____

    _____

13. That's a shame.   I didn't know _____

    _____

14. Are you sure?   I didn't know _____

    _____

15. I don't believe it! I didn't know _____

_____.

16. That's too bad. I didn't know _____

_____.

D. QUESTIONS! QUESTIONS! QUESTIONS!

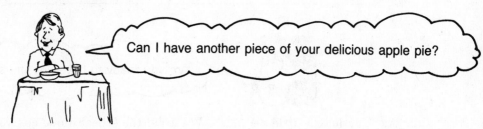

1. A. Jack is a wonderful cook.

   B. Yes, he really is. He was so happy last night when I asked him _____ *(if/whether)*

   _____ *I could have another piece of his delicious pie* _____.

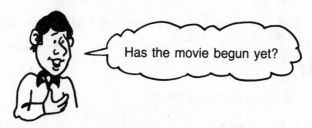

2. A. What did Alan ask the woman at the box office?

   B. I'm not sure. I think he asked her _____

   _____.

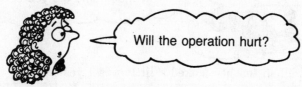

3. A. What did your wife ask Dr. Anderson?

   B. I'm not sure, but she might have asked him _____

   _____.

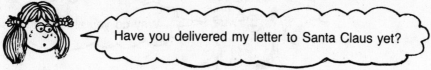

4. A. The mailman looks so surprised! What did your daughter ask him?

   B. She asked him _____

   _____.

(continued)

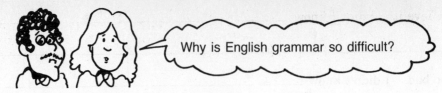

5. A. I think those students look confused.

   B. They are. They asked me _____

   _____

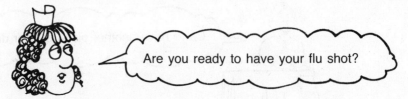

6. A. You look a little nervous. What did the school nurse ask you?

   B. She asked me _____

   _____

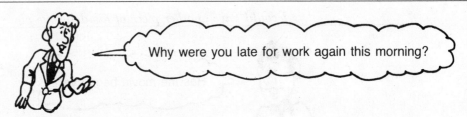

7. A. I think Shirley's boss is upset with her.

   B. I know. He asked her _____

8. A. Your English teacher looked a little upset yesterday.

   B. I know. He asked me _____

   _____

9. A. Did Robert's girlfriend enjoy their drive in the country yesterday?

   B. No, she didn't. She asked him _____

   _____

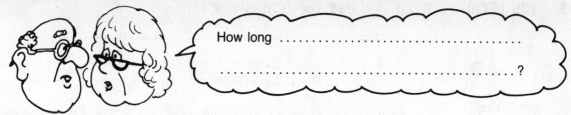

How long ....
....?

10. A. Your parents look very concerned. What did they ask you?

B. They asked me _____

_____.

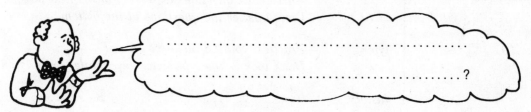

....
....?

11. A. When you were talking to the auto mechanic you really looked annoyed. What did you ask him?

B. I asked him _____

_____.

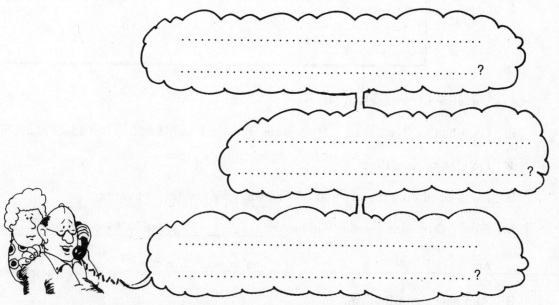

....
....?

....
....?

....
....?

12. A. Our new neighbors called last night, and we talked for hours. They had lots of questions about the building and the neighborhood.

B. Oh? What did they ask you?

A. They asked me

_____,

_____,

and _____.

E. YOU DECIDE: *What We Had for Homework*

math	— *Study Chapters 5 and 7.*
	Don't study Chapter 6.
English	— *Write a composition about any famous English artist.*
	Don't forget to look for grammar mistakes.
French	— *Translate the story on page 36.*
	Don't use a dictionary.
	Answer the questions at the top of the next page.
	Don't answer the questions at the bottom.
typing	— *Practice typing a business letter.*
	Don't look at the typewriter keys while you're typing.
history	— ....
	Don't ....
philosophy — ....
	Don't ....
basketball — ....
	Don't ....

A. We missed you at school last week.   Where were you?

B. Oh, I had to stay in bed.   My mother thought I had the flu.   But I feel much better now.

A. I'm glad to hear that.

B. I was wondering if you could tell me what we had for homework.

A. Sure.   Our math teacher told us _____ *to study Chapters 5 and 7* _____ ¹

and _____ *not to study Chapter 6* _____ ²

B. And how about English?

A. Our English teacher told us _____

_____ ³

and _____ ⁴

B. That sounds difficult.   I hope I can do it.

A. I'm sure you can.

B. Anything else?

A. Yes. Our French teacher told us _____
_____ 5

and _____
_____ . 6

She also told us _____
_____ 7

and _____
_____ . 8

B. That should be easy.   And how about our typing teacher?   What did he say?

A. Our typing teacher told us _____
_____ 9

and _____
_____ . 10

B. Anything else?

A. Well, our history teacher told us _____

_____ 11

and _____
_____ . 12

And our philosophy teacher told us _____

_____ 13

and _____
_____ 14

And our basketball coach told us _____

_____ 15

and _____
_____ . 16

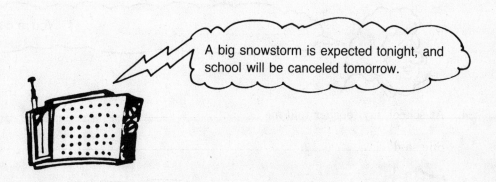

A big snowstorm is expected tonight, and
school will be canceled tomorrow.

B. I don't think I'll ever finish all this homework.

A. Don't worry.   You'll have enough time.   The radio just said _____

_____ . 17

B. I can't believe it!   I'm so glad I called you.   I guess I'll have enough time to do all this
homework after all.

F. EVERYBODY ALWAYS TELLS HIM WHAT TO DO

I'm tired of being told what to do. All day yesterday people did NOTHING ELSE but tell me what to do!

Hurry! Your breakfast is getting cold.

1. As soon as I woke up, my mother told me _____ *to hurry* _____.

   She said _____ *my breakfast was getting cold* _____.

Don't forget your raincoat! It's going to rain today.

2. At breakfast my father told me _____.

   He said _____.

Don't walk so slowly! We'll be late for school.

3. On the way to school, my friend Mark told me _____.

   He said _____.

. . . . ! You're disturbing the class.

4. At school, my teacher told me _____.

   She said _____.

. . . . ! . . . .

5. When we were walking home from school, the policeman on the corner told me _____

   _____.

   He said _____.

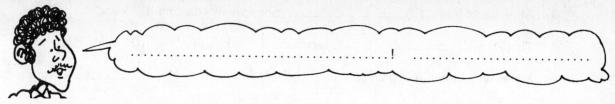

6. At my music lesson, my music teacher told me _____

    _____. He said _____.

 ....! You'll fail your math test if you don't study.

7. I was hoping to watch the football game on TV last night, but my older brother told me

    _____

    _____

    He said _____.

 ....! You have to get up early in the morning for school.

8. I couldn't even choose my own bedtime. My parents told me _____

    _____. They said _____

    _____.

    I can't wait until I grow up! Then I can tell everybody else what to do!

G. WHAT'S THE WORD?

Fill in the blank with the appropriate word.

bride	escaped	irritable	performance	stopped
customers	expect	lonely	rare	tastes
daily	falling in love	low	reach	tired
delivered	flu shot	memory	serious	traffic light
die	go on strike	nephew	shrink	trust
encyclopedia	groom	niece	snowstorm	

1. My mother is always so ___*irritable*___ when my friends and I play rock music in the living room all afternoon.

2. The only girl Ronald ever talks about is Sylvia. I think he's _____ with her.

3. Alice has a bad _____. She can NEVER find her keys!

4. This stew _____ terrible. I think it needs a little more salt.

5. My sister's twins looked so cute at their birthday party. My _____ wore a little blue dress and my _____ wore a little blue suit.

6. The veterinarian said that Fred's parrot had a _____ disease. I hope it doesn't _____.

7. Sharon's grandfather says he looks so young because he does his exercises every morning and takes a _____ walk.

8. Mario didn't know his new shirt would _____ the first time it was washed. It was 100 percent cotton.

9. If my grandmother had had her _____ last fall, she wouldn't have gotten sick this winter.

10. Janet studies hard. I'm surprised she got such a _____ grade.

11. The police _____ all the cars on the highway. I think they're looking for the dangerous robber who _____ from jail last night.

12. Alice had hoped that a lot of people would come to her party, but she certainly didn't _____ EVERYBODY to come!

13. I'll need a ladder to fix your porch light. I can't _____ that high.

14. The workers aren't satisfied because they aren't paid enough. If they don't get paid more, they'll _____.

15. Gregory has been standing on this corner for over an hour. He's really _____ of waiting for the bus.

16. The road has been covered with ice since that last _____.

17. You'll find a lot of information in our twenty-volume _____.

18. Would you please check and see if the mailman has _____ our mail yet?

19. You should always stop your car when you come to a red _____.

20. He's always polite to all the people who come into his store because he wants to keep his _____ happy.

21. That was the worst _____ of my life. Do you think they'll ever ask me to act in one of their plays again?

22. I loved Mark and Sheila's wedding! They were the most attractive _____ and _____ I had ever seen.

23. I wish Janet wouldn't study every night and every weekend.   I think she's much too

_____ about her school work.

24. We never believe anything Larry tells us because we don't _____ him.

25. My parents are very _____ now that all their children have moved away.

 H.   LISTEN

Listen to each word and then say it.

1. <u>St</u>uart
2. <u>st</u>and
3. <u>st</u>upid
4. fanta<u>st</u>ic
5. si<u>st</u>er

1. <u>sk</u>ate
2. <u>sk</u>i
3. <u>sc</u>are
4. a<u>sk</u>
5. di<u>sc</u>overed

1. <u>sp</u>orts
2. <u>sp</u>ring
3. <u>sp</u>ecial
4. e<u>sp</u>ecially
5. ho<u>sp</u>ital

6. that<u>'s</u>
7. patien<u>ts</u>
8. appointmen<u>ts</u>

6. work<u>s</u>
7. think<u>s</u>
8. like<u>s</u>

6. sto<u>ps</u>
7. ski<u>ps</u>
8. hiccu<u>ps</u>

**I.   DR. WEST: _A Very S_ecial Dentis__

Fill in the missing letters and then read aloud.

p	t	k	c

Many pessimis__s don't trus__ dentis__s because they're s__ared the wors__ will happen.

Dr. Wes__'s patien__s, on the other hand, are all optimis__ic.   They think that Dr. Wes__ is the

bes__ dentis__ in Bos__on.

1. S__uart li__es Dr. Wes__.

He isn't only hones__, but he's the cheapes__ and the mos__ reliable
dentis__ in Bos__on.

(continued)   99

2. S__uar__'s sis__er also thin__s Dr. Wes__ is wonderful.

Dr. Wes__ wor__s very fas__ and never ma__es mis__akes. He's the bes__ dentis__ on S__ate S__reet.

3. Mr. Jac__son can't s__and any other dentis__.

I go to Dr. Wes__ because I almos__ never feel any pain when I'm in his office. I could s__ay and res__ in his s__ecial dentis__'s chair all day.

4. Be__sy always tal__s about Dr. Wes__.

What I like mos__ about Dr. Wes__ is that he doesn't as__ a lot of questions when a patien__'s mouth is full of dental ins__rumen__s.

5. Dr. Wes__'s S__anish-s__eaking patien__s are es__ecially pleased.

Dr. Wes__ s__udies S__panish in his s__are time. We won't see any other s__ecialis__ but Dr. Wes__.

6. Margaret is very enthusias__ic about Dr. Wes__.

The day I got the hiccu__s in his office, Dr. Wes__ jus__ s__opped and s__ood there waiting patiently. He didn't make me feel s__upid at all!

7. Patty thin__s Dr. Wes__ is the hardes__ working dentis__ she knows.

Dr. Wes__ never qui__s working all day. He even s__ips his lunch!

8. S__eve also li__es Dr. Wes__.

When I s__rained my ankle playing bas__etball las__ s__ring, I missed two appointmen__s. Dr. Wes__ wasn't u__set at all. He even visited me in the hos__ital. We dis__ussed politi__s and s__orts. Tha__'s when I dis__overed that Dr. Wes__ li__es to s__i and s__ate.

All of Dr. Wes__'s patien__s agree that he's a fantas__ic dentis__!

100

A. WHAT ARE THEY SAYING?

1. This is the first time you've given blood, _____*isn't it*_____?

2. We just flew over Paris, _____?

3. Dinner will be ready soon, _____?

4. We can stop and get something to eat now, _____?

5. Your son-in-law works at a bank, _____?

6. We've eaten at this restaurant before, _____?

7. Santa Claus will be here in a little while, _____?

8. We have to go to bed now, _____?

9. Apples are on sale this week, _____?

10. You were on the bus tour with us this morning, _____?

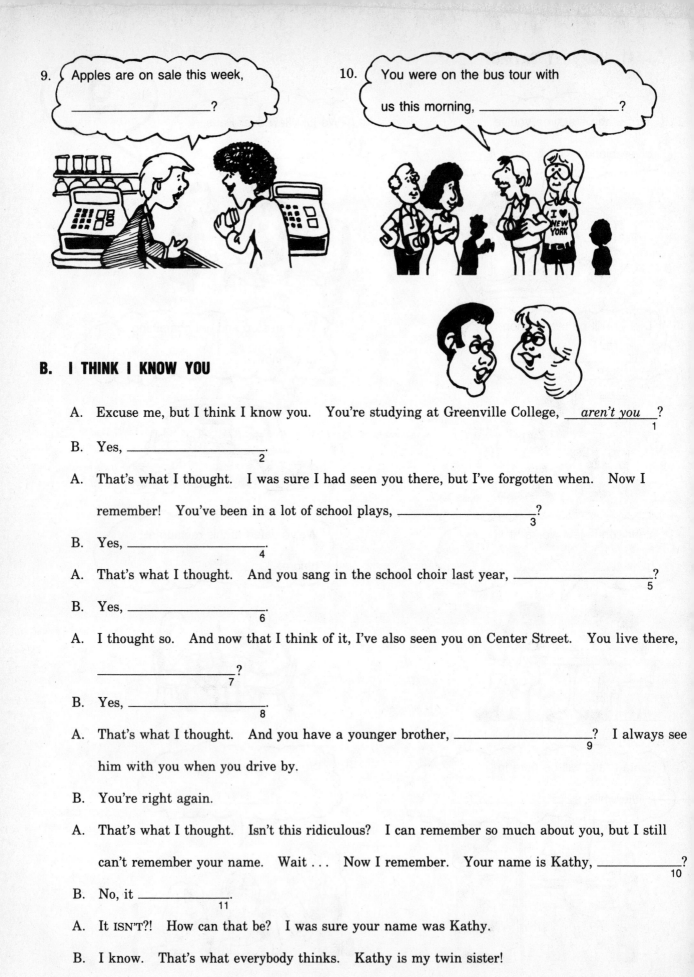

B. I THINK I KNOW YOU

A. Excuse me, but I think I know you. You're studying at Greenville College, *aren't you*₁?

B. Yes, _____₂.

A. That's what I thought. I was sure I had seen you there, but I've forgotten when. Now I remember! You've been in a lot of school plays, _____₃?

B. Yes, _____₄.

A. That's what I thought. And you sang in the school choir last year, _____₅?

B. Yes, _____₆.

A. I thought so. And now that I think of it, I've also seen you on Center Street. You live there, _____₇?

B. Yes, _____₈.

A. That's what I thought. And you have a younger brother, _____₉? I always see him with you when you drive by.

B. You're right again.

A. That's what I thought. Isn't this ridiculous? I can remember so much about you, but I still can't remember your name. Wait ... Now I remember. Your name is Kathy, _____₁₀?

B. No, it _____₁₁.

A. It ISN'T?! How can that be? I was sure your name was Kathy.

B. I know. That's what everybody thinks. Kathy is my twin sister!

102

C. THAT'S WHAT I THOUGHT

When I woke up yesterday morning, I knew right away it was going to be a terrible day.   I knew that EVERYTHING was going to go wrong ALL DAY, and that I couldn't do ANYTHING about it.

My problems started the minute I got up.

1. A.   Breakfast isn't ready yet, _____*is it*_____?

    B.   No, _____*it isn't*_____.

    A.   That's what I thought.

2. A.   I don't have time to take a shower, _____?

    B.   No, _____.

    A.   That's what I thought.

3. A.   I lost my English book.   You haven't seen it anywhere, _____?

    B.   No, _____.

    A.   That's what I thought.

4. A.   There isn't any more orange juice, _____?

    B.   No, _____.

    A.   That's what I thought.

5. A.   Mother hasn't ironed my shirt yet, _____?

    B.   No, _____.

    A.   That's what I thought.

6. A.   I won't be able to finish my breakfast, _____?

    B.   No, _____.

    A.   That's what I thought.

7. A.   We're going to be late for school, _____?

    B.   Yes, _____.

    A.   That's what I thought.

(continued)

I had even more problems at school.

8. A. The English test wasn't canceled, _____?

   B. No, _____.

   A. That's what I thought.

9. A. I can't hand in today's homework assignment next week, _____?

   B. No, _____.

   A. That's what I thought.

10. A. They're serving spinach for lunch today, _____?

    B. Yes, _____.

    A. That's what I thought.

11. A. You didn't like my history composition very much, _____?

    B. No, _____.

    A. That's what I thought.

12. A. The math teacher was angry at me, _____?

    B. Yes, _____.

    A. That's what I thought.

And I had even more problems when I got home.

What a terrible day!

D. LISTEN

Listen and complete the sentences.

Ex. a. , _____*don't you*_____ ?

   b. , _____*are you*_____ ?

1. , _____ ?   5. , _____ ?   9. , _____
2. , _____ ?   6. , _____ ?   10. , _____
3. , _____ ?   7. , _____ ?   11. , _____
4. , _____ ?   8. , _____ ?   12. , _____

E. SURPRISES

1. A. You haven't been waiting long, ____*have you*____?

   B. I'm afraid ____*I have*____.

   A. ____*You have*____?! I'm really sorry. I had no idea it was so late.

2. A. Richard is going to medical school next year, _____?

   B. No, _____.

   A. _____?! I thought he wanted to be a doctor just like his father.

3. A. Albert won't be at your party tomorrow, _____?

   B. Yes, _____.

   A. _____?! I can't believe you decided to invite him.

4. A. Our spring vacation begins tomorrow, _____?

   B. No, _____.

   A. _____?! You must be kidding! I've been looking forward to tomorrow all month.

5. A. It's time to eat. You brought the sandwiches, _____?

   B. Sandwiches?! No, _____.

   A. _____?! How could you have forgotten? I was sure you were going to bring them.

6. A. Johnny doesn't go to high school yet, _____?

   B. I know it's hard to believe, but _____.

   A. _____?! I can remember when he was just learning how to read. Children grow up so quickly.

F. HIGH SCHOOL REUNION

1. A. Do you ever see our old friend Susan? She was one of the nicest people in our class.

   B. I sure do. As a matter of fact, I married her.

   A. _____*You did*_____?! I don't believe it! You _____*didn't*_____ really _____*marry*_____ Susan, _____*did you*_____?

2. A. Do you still go dancing every weekend?

   B. Not anymore. I'm MUCH too busy. I have three small children at home.

   A. _____?! I NEVER would have believed it!

   You _____ really _____ three children,

   _____?

3. A. Do you still work for the PRESTO Company?

   B. Yes. As a matter of fact, I'm the president.

   A. _____?! I don't believe it! You _____

   really _____ of the PRESTO Company,

   _____?

4. A. Have you heard from your old friend Carol recently?

   B. Yes, and I have some good news. She's been ....

   ....

   A. _____?! That's wonderful.

5. A. Have you heard? Charlie Parker quit his job and ....

....

B. _____?! I can't believe it! He _____

really _____, _____?

6. A. Has anybody heard from Gregory? I wonder what ever happened to him.

B. Well, the last time I saw him he was ....

....

A. _____?! I'm really surprised.

7. A. Tell me about your son Willy. I hear he's a very special little boy.

B. You don't really want to hear about Willy, _____?

A. Yes. I'm VERY interested.

B. Well, Willy is only four years old, but he can ....

....,

and ....

A. _____?! I don't believe it! He _____

really do ALL those things, _____?

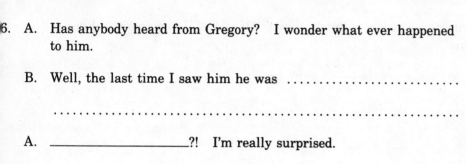

8. A. How's little Patty?

B. My daughter Patty isn't so little anymore. She's going to

.... next month.

A. _____?! I don't believe it! She _____

really going to _____ next month,

_____? She was just a baby the last time I saw her.

G. YOU DECIDE: *Why Shouldn't They Break Up?*

A. I'm going to break up with my boyfriend, Harold.

B. I don't believe it! Why do you want to break up with Harold? He's a wonderful person. He's kind and generous.

A. I guess he ___*IS*___ kind and generous, ___*isn't he*___ .
           1   2

B. And he sends you flowers all the time.

A. Come to think of it, he _____ _____ me flowers all the time, _____
                                  3   4   5

B. And he's . . . .
         6

A. I guess you're right. He _____
                         7

_____ .
        8

B. And remember how happy you were last month when Harold bought you . . . .

. . . .
          9

A. Come to think of it, he _____ _____ me _____
                               10   11   12

last month, _____ . And I _____ very happy, _____
                    13   14   15

B. Yes. But to tell the truth, I wasn't very surprised, because he's always given you a lot of presents.

A. That's true. He _____ always _____ me a lot of presents, _____
                     16   17   18

B. And here's something else to think about. He doesn't . . . .

. . . .
          19

A. You're right. He _____ , _____
                                     20   21

B. Also, ...
          22

A. Come to think of it, that's true. _____

_____ , _____
                                 23   24

B. And how do you think Harold would feel? He'd be VERY upset if you broke up with him.

A. I'm afraid you're right. He _____ be very upset, _____
                                   25   26

You know . . . I'm really glad I talked to you. I guess I won't break up with Harold after all.

108

H. YOU DECIDE: *A Good Father*

I can't understand why I've been having so many problems with my teenage son. After all,

I'm a good father, _____*aren't I*_____?
1

I try to be patient, _____?
2

I'm nice to his friends, _____?
3

I've always .... , _____?
4   5

When he was little, I .... , _____?
6   7

And now that he's older, I ....

.... , _____?
8   9

I'm not .... , _____?
10   11

I don't .... , _____?
12   13

I'm always there when he needs me, _____?
14
So what could have gone wrong?

 I. LISTEN

Listen to each word and then say it.

1. boat	1. vote	1. won't
2. better	2. vet	2. weather
3. about	3. avoid	3. away
4. been	4. oven	4. window
5. trouble	5. travel	5. tower
6. bright	6. advice	6. twice
7. garbage	7. nervous	7. sandwich
8. job	8. love	8. worry

Beverly Wilson's typewriter is broken. The b's, v's and w's don't always work. Fill in the missing b's, v's, and w's, and then read Beverly's letters aloud.

1.

Dear __etty,
   You'__e pro__a__ly heard from Bo__ a__out the terri__le
ro__ __eries __e'__e __een ha__ing in our neighborhood. (There ha__e
__een se__en ro__ __eries in fi__e __eeks!) Of course, e__ery__ody's
__een __ery __orried __ecause they still ha__en't disco__ered
who the ro__ __ers __ere.
   Last __ednesday my neigh__or __incent's __icycle __as stolen from
his __asement. The next e__ening some__ody __roke into a __uilding
on __righton __oule__ard and took se__eral sil__er __racelets,
a __allet, and a T__.
   Then last __eekend, __elie__e it or not, the Relia__le __ank __as
ro__ __ed. I'll al__ays remem__er the e__ening of the ro__ __ery.
I __as taking a __ath, and my hus__and, __ill, __as reading his
fa__orite no__el in __ed __hen Ro__er __egan __arking. He must
ha__e heard the ro__ __er dri__ing a__ay. __y the time I got out
of the __athtu__, e__ery__ody in the neigh__orhood __as talking
a__out the ro__ __er's escape.
   __ell, e__er since the __ank ro__ __ery last __eekend, __e'__e all
__een __ery ner__ous. Some of the neigh__ors are so __orried that
they're e__en thinking a__out mo__ing a__ay. __ill and I ha__e __een
__ondering __hat __e should do.

                        Lo__e,
                        __e__erly

2.

Dear __etsy,

__e're ha__ing a __edding anni__ersary cele__ration on __ednesday for my __rother-in-law __arney and his wife, Ro__erta, and __e __ould lo__e it if you and your hus__and, __alter, __ere there. It __on't __e a __ery __ig cele__ration, just a few relati__es, __illiam, __incent, Eliza__eth, Ste__e, and of course my __rothers and their __i__es.

__e'__e heard that your __rother's little __oy __o__y is __isiting you this __eek. __hy don't you __ring him along __ith you __hen you come o__er on __ednesday?

Lo__e,
__e__erly

3.

Dear Al__ert,

__e're ha__ing a __onderful time on our __acation in __oston, __ut __e __ish you and your __ife __ere here __ith us.

I'm positi__e __oth you and __ar__ara __ould lo__e it here. __ar__ara __ould lo__e the __oston Pu__lic Garden and the __oats on the Charles Ri__er. And you __ould ha__e a __onderful time __isiting the uni__ersities and the __oston Pu__lic Li__rary.

__e're staying __ith __ill's relati__es __hile __e're in __oston. They li__e in a __ery modern high-rise __uilding __ith a __eautiful __iew of the ri__er. __e'__e __een __ery lucky. __ill's relati__es dri__e us e__ery__here.

The __eather in __oston __as __ery __arm __hen __e arri__ed, but now it's __indy. I __ish __e had __rought __armer clothes to __ear.

__y the __ay, __ill and I __ent to a li__ely __ase__all game last __ednesday, and __e'__e __een to the __oston __allet t__ice. __e'__e also __een __ery __usy __uying presents for e__ery__ody at home and sou__enirs for oursel__es. (__e __eren't a__le to __uy the __atch your __rother __alter __anted.)

Next __eek __e're tra__eling __y __us to __ashington, D.C.

__e're looking for__ard to seeing you in Septem__er. __e'll pro__a__ly __e __ack on the ele__enth or the t__elfth. __e hope you'__e __oth __een __ell.

Lo__e,
__e__erly

A. WHAT ARE THEY SAYING?

see

1. A. Do you really want _____*to see*_____ a movie again tonight? I know you enjoy
      _____ movies, but you've already _____ four movies this week, and you
              2   3
      just _____ a movie this afternoon. Don't you EVER get tired of _____
              4   5
      movies? If I were you, I certainly _____ another movie tonight.
                                                      6

   B. Maybe I'm a little crazy, but there's nothing I like more than _____ movies. I
                                                                              7
      really DO feel like _____ a movie with you tonight, and believe it or not, I'm
                                  8
      planning _____ another movie tomorrow!
                      9

worry

2. A. I'm really concerned about you, Frieda. You worry too much. Whenever I see you, you're
      _____. You start _____ as soon as you get up in the morning, and
              1   2
      you keep on _____ until you go to bed at night. You _____ while you're
                          3   4
      working, you _____ while you're driving, and you even _____ while you're
                          5   6
      eating! Listen to me, Frieda. You've _____ since the day I met you.
                                                          7
      You've really got to quit _____. _____ all the time is very bad for
                                        8   9
      your health.

   B. Don't worry about me. It's true that I _____ a lot, but I'm not very worried that
                                                      10
      _____ is bad for my health.
              11

112

| do |

3. I don't feel like _____ the dishes again tonight.   I've _____ the dishes
         1   2

EVERY day this week, and I'm really tired of _____ them.   I'd be happy
                                              3

_____ the dishes some other time, but NOT tonight.   By the way, Mary never
        4

_____ the dishes, and she's only a few years younger than I am.   Don't you think
        5

she should start _____ the dishes soon?   Come to think of it, Mary would probably
                      6

enjoy _____ the dishes.   After all, she LOVES water, and she LOVES taking baths!
           7

| go |

4. A. We're _____ hiking this weekend.   Would you like to come with us?
                1

   B. I don't think so.   To be honest, I don't really like _____ hiking.
                                                              2

   A. You DON'T?!   I thought you _____ hiking all the time.
                                     3

   B. That's true, but it's only because everybody else in my family loves _____ hiking.
                                                                             4

      If you really want to know the truth, I CAN'T STAND _____ hiking!   Ever since I
                                                             5

      first _____ hiking years ago, I've HATED it!   If my family didn't enjoy
               6

      _____ hiking so much, _____ NEVER _____ hiking at all!
            7   8   9

   A. I'm sorry you feel that way.   I'll never ask you _____ hiking again.
                                                          10

113

B. YOU DECIDE: *I'm Really Sorry*

1. You've been stopped by a police
    officer because you just went
    through a red light.

    Police Officer: You just drove through a red light.   Didn't you see it?

    You: ....

    ....

    ....

    Police Officer: ....

    ....

    ....

    You: ....

    ....

2. Last night, you and your wife had a
    big party.   All of your friends were there.
    You had no idea your neighbor was trying to
    study for an important exam.

    Your neighbor: I'm very upset.   While you were having your party last night, I was trying to
    study.   But I couldn't concentrate with all that noise.

    You: ....

    ....

    ....

    Your neighbor: ....

    ....

    ....

    You: ....

    ....

114

3. You and your two-year-old
   son are at a friend's house.
   Your son just ripped up an
   important business letter and
   poured ink all over your
   friend's expensive rug.

Your friend: My letter!!   My rug!!   What am I going to do?!

You: ....

....

....

Your friend: ....

....

You: ....

....

4. You're having dinner at a
   friend's house, and you just
   ate the last piece of cake.

Your friend: I think I'll have some cake now.   I haven't tried it yet.

You: ....

....

....

Your friend: ....

....

You: ....

....

5. You and your friends have been playing baseball all afternoon. You've just hit the ball very hard, and when you look to see where it's gone, you realize you've broken a neighbor's window.

Your neighbor: Look what you've done!   How could you be so careless?!

You: ....

....

....

Your neighbor: ....

....

....

You: ....

....

6. You've been invited to a party. You arrive on the wrong day. Your friends are cleaning the house.

Your friends: What a nice surprise!   As you can see, we're getting ready for tomorrow's party.

You: ....

....

....

Your friends: ....

....

....

You: ....

....

C. LISTEN

Listen to each word and then say it.

1. b<u>a</u>d – b<u>e</u>d
2. l<u>a</u>dder – l<u>e</u>tter
3. s<u>a</u>d – s<u>ai</u>d
4. b<u>oa</u>t – b<u>ou</u>ght

5. c<u>oa</u>t – c<u>au</u>ght
6. f<u>oo</u>t – f<u>oo</u>d
7. g<u>o</u>ne – g<u>u</u>n
8. l<u>o</u>ck – l<u>u</u>ck

9. h<u>i</u>t – h<u>ea</u>t
10. s<u>e</u>ll – s<u>ai</u>l
11. w<u>o</u>n't – w<u>a</u>nt

D. HAVE YOU HEARD?

Listen and complete the sentences.

sell	sail

1. a. . . . away across the ocean.
   b. . . . his old car.

letter	ladder

2. a. . . . I'll mail it.
   b. . . . I'll be able to reach the broken window.

lock	luck

3. a. . . . on my test.
   b. . . . for my door.

hit	heat

4. a. . . . the building because it's cold.
   b. . . . the ball.

foot	food

5. a. . . . is ready. I'm going to eat.
   b. . . . hurts.

bad	bed

6. a. . . . isn't made.
   b. . . . grades aren't getting better.

sad	said

7. a. . . . she was going to be busy today.
   b. . . . because her boyfriend moved away.

boss	bus

8. a. . . . didn't stop at every corner.
   b. . . . had given me a raise.

coat	caught

9. a. . . . a very big fish.
   b. . . . looks very comfortable.

boat	bought

10. a. . . . a new house.
    b. . . . makes me seasick.

won't	want

11. a. . . . be able to go skiing tomorrow.
    b. . . . to go dancing tonight.

gone	gun

12. a. . . . was stolen.
    b. . . . away.

coat	caught

13. a. . . . is very warm.
    b. . . . a bad cold.

boss	bus

14. a. . . ., has he?
    b. . . ., has it?

won't	want

15. a. . . . to get a good grade.
    b. . . . have time to finish my test.

foot	food

16. a. . . . has been hurting him recently.
    b. . . . looks delicious.

(continued) 117

ladder	letter

17. a. ... I just wrote?
    b. ... I borrowed when I was fixing the roof?

hit	heat

18. a. ... the ball so hard.
    b. ... your apartment today. It's warm outside.

E. WHAT DOES IT MEAN?

apology	customers	ice	nephew
arrested	daily	lake	niece
audience	deaf	legibly	nutritious
carve	deliver	list	offend
chase	detergent	lock	penicillin
choose	escape	mail	robber
clog	expect	mayor	shampoo
communicate	hide	native language	shrink
concern			wedding anniversary

1. _____*list*_____ : names of things written one after another

2. _____ : large pond

3. _____ : run after

4. _____ : people shopping at a store

5. _____ : cut or slice meat

6. _____ : pick out

7. _____ : worry, serious care

8. _____ : get away, get free

9. _____ : stopped and held by a policeman

10. _____ : people watching a performance

11. _____ : every day

12. _____ : letters and packages

13. _____ : get smaller

14. _____ : put something where it can't be seen

15. _____ : a celebration on the date someone was married

16. _____ : not able to hear

17. _____ : laundry soap

18. _____ : give and receive information

19. _____ : stop water from going through

20. _____ : take packages and letters to someone

21. _____ : an elected manager of a city

22. _____ : frozen water

23. _____ : neatly (when talking about writing)

24. _____ : someone who steals

25. _____ : the language you learned as a child

26. _____ : say or do something to make someone unhappy or upset

27. _____ : soap for hair

28. _____ : healthy to eat

29. _____ : son of your brother or sister

30. _____ : daughter of your brother or sister

31. _____ : what you say when you're sorry

32. _____ : close with a key

33. _____ : a cure for many diseases

34. _____ : think something will happen

F. BAD CONNECTIONS

1.

I'm angry at you because ########

I'm sorry. We have a bad connection.

*Why are you mad at me* ?

2.

If there are any problems while we're away, please write to us. We'll be staying at #########

Excuse me. I can't hear you. _____

_____

_____ ?

(continued) 119

G. WHAT'S THE WORD?

1. I'm going to be out [of / from / for] town, so I won't be able to see you this weekend.

2. I don't know whether your car is ready. Why don't you check [at / to / with] the mechanic?

3. You've been complaining all day. You're [on / in / at] a terrible mood, aren't you.

4. I can't reach [to / – / at] the cookie jar. It's too high.

5. How can you concentrate [at / in / on] your homework while you're watching TV?

6. I've been sneezing all morning. I must be allergic [at / to / for] something.

7. Marvin won't have any free time when he's in Paris next month. He's being sent [to / in / on] business.

8. Brian is very pleased [with / to / on] his new apartment. It has a beautiful view [of / to / for] the river.

9. We've been studying prepositions for months, and we're getting tired [on / of / for] them!

10. Do you [by / for / from] any chance know what time the movie begins?

11. No wonder Diane and Alan don't get along [to / for / with] each other! They don't have anything [in / on / at] common.

12. We're going crazy! The elevator has been out [from / of / in] order all week.

13. Come to think
[of / on / to]
it, I DID drive
[along / across / through]
a red light, didn't I. I must have had my mind
[at / to / on]
something else.

14. Charlie doesn't usually wear a suit and tie, but he's dressed
[on / up / out]
today.

15. The workers aren't satisfied
[with / on / at]
their new contract. They're going to go
[at / in / on]
strike.

16. My son and daughter went skiing
[for / at / on]
the first time last weekend.

17. Mrs. Rinaldi was taken to the hospital
[for / by / with]
ambulance. Her neighbors are very concerned
[on / from / about]
her.

18. The ice cream truck drives
[at / by / through]
our house every day.

19. David got
[into / – / at]
a terrible argument with his sister, and I had to break
[out / up / in]
the fight.

20. If you drop
[off / – / out]
of school, you're going to wind
[out / with / up]
regretting it.

21. I'll be happy to take care
[for / of / to]
the children when you and your husband go away
[at / – / for]
the weekend.

22. There's no question
[at / by / in]
my mind. We shouldn't have invited your boss to the party. I'm sure he felt out
[from / – / of]
place.

122

23. Could you pick

on
up
off

some tomatoes at the store? They're

on
at
in

sale this week. I'd buy

them myself, but I'm

on
in
at

a hurry.

24. I can't decide whether I should buy my son a chemistry set for his birthday. I know he's very

interested

with
in
on

chemistry and he'd probably learn a lot if he had one.

In
On
At

the other

hand, he might blow

up
out
on

our house or set it

to
on
of

fire!

H. I FEEL TERRIBLE

call up	drop off	hang up
clean up	fill out	pick up

I feel terrible. I've been so busy working overtime these past months that I haven't been able to do ANYTHING else.

I can't believe how dirty my apartment is! I haven't ___cleaned___ ___it___ ___up___ since my little nephew came to visit last September.

1   2   3

My mother must be very upset. The last time I saw her, I told her I'd

_____ _____ _____ every week. (Mother loves to talk on the telephone.)

4   5   6

But I haven't had the time.

And Aunt Gertrude keeps asking when I'm going to hang up her portrait. I hope

she isn't offended because I _____ _____ _____ _____ yet.

7   8   9   10

Also, my best suits have been at the cleaner's since I _____ _____

11   12

_____ months ago. If I don't _____ _____ _____, they might get lost.

13   14   15   16

But tonight when I get home, I'm not going to do ANY of these things. Instead, I'm

going to start _____ _____ the job application from the PRESTO Company.

17   18

I think it's time to find an easier job with less overtime.

I. WHAT'S THE WORD?

alone	contact lenses	hit	pocket
anniversary	dangerous	misunderstood	realized
application	daydreams	news	replace
bank loan	earth	offended	unemployed
championship	faucet	out of order	waiter
congratulations	flat	pills	wallpaper

1. Mary had been my college roommate for two months before we _____*realized*_____ that we were from the same town.

2. Please drive carefully! This narrow street is very _____ in the dark.

3. My daughter Alice is a fantastic athlete. She just won the school tennis _____ again.

4. The plumber said we needed a new hot water _____ in the bathtub, and the painter said we needed new _____ in the bedroom. I think we'll have to get a _____ to pay for all these repairs!

5. This is a wonderful party, but I really DO have to leave early. I hope you won't be _____.

6. Tony must have looked at himself in the mirror twenty times today. He can't decide whether he looks better in glasses or in _____.

7. Peter hopes to find a job soon. He hates being _____.

8. I think you must have _____ me. I never said I didn't like your sister.

9. We can't do the laundry today because our washing machine is _____.

10. I wasn't lonely when I lived by myself last summer. I enjoyed living _____.

11. Johnny is in trouble with his teacher again. She says he _____ instead of paying attention in class.

12. Did your doctor tell you to take these little yellow _____ for your allergy?

13. I didn't know your brother was a _____. Does he work in the same restaurant as you?

14. I miss the mountains where I grew up. This part of the country is too _____.

15. Tom had to fill out an _____ before he went for a job interview.

16. That refrigerator is so old. I really think we should _____ it with a new one.

17. Sally has always wanted to be an astronaut.   She thinks it would be exciting to look down on the _____ from the moon.

18. Have you heard the bad _____?   The President is talking about raising taxes again.

19. We're taking my parents to a fancy restaurant for dinner.   They've been married for twenty years, and today is their _____.

20. Jack had another accident with his son's toy airplane.   This time he was flying it too low, and it _____ a tree.

21. _____!   My son told me you were elected president of your class.

J. LISTEN: *Bad Advice*

Read the questions and then listen to the passage.   Then answer the questions.

JANE'S PROBLEM

1. What advice did Jane's friend give her?   _____
_____

2. What happened when Jane followed her friend's advice?   _____
_____

3. Why wasn't Jane's boss satisfied with her work?   _____
_____

JENNIFER AND NORMAN

1. What advice did Jennifer's parents give her?   _____
_____

2. Why?   _____
_____

3. Why is Jennifer happy she married Norman?   _____
_____

4. Why isn't Jennifer worried about her sons?   _____
_____

K. OUT OF PLACE

Put a circle around the word that doesn't belong.

1.	performance	(perfume)	play	actor	audience
2.	snowman	mailman	stewardess	waiter	librarian
3.	frozen	ice	snowstorm	whether	freeze
4.	movie star	fan	film	box office	telescope
5.	lake	pond	ocean	poodle	river
6.	encyclopedia	typewriter	dictionary	novel	magazine
7.	astronomy	chemistry	apology	history	philosophy
8.	high-rise	nature	hiking	skiing	mountains
9.	sonata	anthem	encore	drum	rubber band
10.	depressed	discovered	disappointed	in a bad mood	under the weather
11.	dolphin	parrot	cactus	elephant	lion
12.	mayors	senators	vice-presidents	agents	congressmen
13.	escape	chase	arrest	gun	bank loan
14.	faucets	typing paper	ink	paper clips	envelopes
15.	capable	reliable	accurate	experienced	nutritious
16.	dance teacher	coach	customer	professor	ski instructor
17.	mention	say	tell	considerate	communicate
18.	emergency	application	ambulance	crash	drown
19.	annoyed	irritable	angry	mad	confused
20.	unemployed	fired	retired	promoted	out of work

 **L. LISTEN**

Listen to each word and then say it.

1. b<u>l</u>ush – b<u>r</u>ush
2. <u>l</u>ight – <u>r</u>ight
3. <u>l</u>ong – <u>wr</u>ong
4. bo<u>y</u>s – <u>v</u>oice
5. <u>ch</u>op – <u>sh</u>op
6. <u>ch</u>opping – <u>sh</u>opping
7. wat<u>ch</u> – wa<u>sh</u>
8. hear<u>d</u> – hur<u>t</u>

9. ri<u>d</u>e – wri<u>t</u>e
10. ri<u>dd</u>en – wri<u>tt</u>en
11. sen<u>d</u> – sen<u>t</u>
12. wi<u>d</u>e – whi<u>t</u>e
13. so<u>m</u>eday – Su<u>n</u>day
14. war<u>m</u> – wor<u>n</u>
15. ru<u>n</u> – ru<u>ng</u>

 **M. HAVE YOU HEARD?**

Listen and complete the sentences.

watch	wash

1. a. . . . my shirt? It's dirty.

   b. . . . TV?

light	right

2. a. . . . I agree with you.

   b. . . . just went out. It's dark in here.

126

someday	Sunday

3. a. . . . is my favorite day of the week.

   b. . . . I'll be rich and famous.

wide	white

4. a. . . . or narrow?

   b. . . . or yellow?

ride	write

5. a. . . . you a long letter.

   b. . . . my bicycle to school.

long	wrong

6. a. . . ., but I can't find my mistake.

   b. It's more than 3 pages.

run	rung

7. a. . . . in a marathon.

   b. . . . the bells.

boys	voice

8. a. . . . is beautiful.   I love to hear you sing.

   b. . . . are wonderful children.

warm	worn

9. a. . . . yet.   It's new.

   b. . . . enough to wear on the coldest days.

light	right

10. a. I can lift it easily.

    b. Your answer is fine.

watch	wash

11. a. . . . my favorite TV program.

    b. . . . the dishes.

heard	hurt

12. a. . . . about Janet?

    b. . . . your leg?

wide	white

13. a. . . . because I painted it that color.

    b. . . ., but our kitchen is narrow.

chopping	shopping

14. a. . . . onions.

    b. . . . at the supermarket.

boys	voice

15. a. . . . are my nephews.

    b. . . . is better than mine.

send	sent

16. a. . . . a letter last week.

    b. . . . letters when they have time.

blushed	brushed

17. a. . . . her teeth this morning.

    b. . . . because she was embarrassed.

chop	shop

18. a. . . . at Wilson's Department Store.

    b. . . . vegetables with a good knife.

heard	hurt

19. a. . . . my arm.

    b. . . . from Margaret recently.

ridden	written

20. a. . . . your motorcycle?

    b. . . . to your uncle?

blushes	brushes

21. a. . . . his teeth before he goes to bed.

    b. . . . when he makes mistakes.

warm	worn

22. a. . . . by a famous actress.

    b. . . . enough to wear on the coldest days.

CHECK-UP TEST: *Chapters 8–10*

A. Complete the sentences.

Ex. Betty was in school yesterday, _____*wasn't she*_____?

1. Your brother sent us a postcard, _____?

2. The train hasn't arrived yet, _____?

3. We can have dinner now, _____?

4. You didn't forget to buy the ice cream, _____?

5. Your daughter studies English, _____?

6. You'll be finished in a little while, _____?

7. You're new in town, _____?

8. Your parents won't be at home this afternoon, _____?

9. I'm a good husband, _____?

10. She's been invited to the party, _____?

B. Complete the sentences.

Ex. (I'm going to buy a new car.)

My brother called yesterday. He said _____*he was going to buy a new car*_____.

1. (Have you studied today's lesson?)

My teacher asked me _____.

2. (Why can't I stay up until midnight?)

My son asked me _____.

3. (I'm sorry I forgot your anniversary.)

Our daughter called yesterday. She said _____

_____.

4. (Brush your teeth every morning, and don't eat any candy.)

My dentist told me _____

_____.

5. (We won't be able to visit you this weekend, but we'll see you next week.)

Fred and Barbara called yesterday. They said _____

us this weekend, but _____.

6. (When will I be old enough to go out on dates?)

   My son asked me _____.

7. (I can't help you with your homework because I don't understand it either.)

   My friend called yesterday. She said _____

   _____.

8. (Do your homework over, and don't make any mistakes this time.)

   My teacher told me _____

C. Write the question.

    Ex. I've decided to <u>drop out of school</u>.   *What have you decided to do*   ?

    1. They'll be staying <u>at the</u>   _____?
        <u>Greenville Hotel</u>.

    2. I lost my wallet <u>a few days ago</u>.   _____?

    3. I've been driving <u>all afternoon</u>.   _____?

    4. He spent <u>forty dollars</u>.   _____?

    5. She's looking for a new job <u>because</u>   _____?
        <u>she doesn't get paid enough</u>.

D. Fill in the blanks.

see

I don't really feel like _____ a movie again tonight. I usually enjoy _____
                                   1   2

movies, but I've already _____ four movies this week, and I just _____ a very
                                         3   4

boring movie last night. If I _____ so many movies this week, I'd be happy
                                                 5

to go to the movies with you.

E. Listen and complete the sentences.

  Ex. Really? I didn't know   *your son wanted to be a doctor*

    1. Really? I didn't know _____.

    2. I don't believe it! I didn't know _____.

    3. That's wonderful! I didn't know _____.

    4. I'm glad to hear that. I didn't know _____.

    5. What a shame! I didn't know _____.

TAPE SCRIPTS FOR LISTENING EXERCISES

Page 5 Exercise F

Listen and fill in the missing words.

Ernest Hemingway is considered one of the most important modern American writers. He has written six novels and more than 50 short stories. He has also written many poems and newspaper articles.

Hemingway's books are lively and exciting. They are full of fighting, traveling, sports, love, and war. Hemingway's life was also lively and exciting.

When he was a young high school student, Hemingway played football, boxed, and wrote for the school newspaper. He ran away from home when he was 15 years old, but he returned and finished high school in 1917. He never went to college.

Hemingway wanted to fight in World War I, but he was rejected by the army. Instead, he went to the war as an ambulance driver and was badly injured.

In 1921 Hemingway went to Paris and started writing seriously. He stayed there for 6 years. His first novel, *The Sun Also Rises*, was written when he was still in Paris. It made him very famous.

In 1937 Hemingway went to Spain as a journalist to write about the Spanish Civil War.

In 1944 he returned to Europe and wrote newspaper articles about World War II. He wasn't in the army during the Second World War, but it's believed that he did more fighting than writing, just the same.

Page 14 Exercise C

Listen and put a circle around the correct answer.

1. Did your husband send you a lot of love letters before you were married?
2. Does Julia have a lot of old furniture in her basement?
3. Did Jack have any problems with his new computer?
4. Could I possibly use some of your medicine for my sore throat?
5. Did you make a lot of mistakes typing all those business letters?
6. Would you care for some more of my Aunt Martha's famous apple pie?
7. Did Harry miss any work when he was sick?
8. Did a lot of people come to visit you when you were in the hospital?
9. Do you need any help with your chemistry homework?
10. Do you need any gas for your motorcycle?
11. Can I borrow some laundry detergent to use at the laundromat?
12. Could I take a few days off work to go skiing next week?

Page 22 Exercise C

Listen to each question. Put a circle around the correct answer.

Ex. Do you want some more salt?

1. Do you want any butter on your cheese sandwich?
2. Have you sent a lot of invitations?
3. Have you spent a lot of time painting your porch?
4. I forgot. Did you want me to buy some typing paper at the store?
5. Do you usually get a lot of telephone calls from your boyfriend?
6. Did you take any days off from work last month?
7. Is there any leftover spaghetti?
8. May I have some more chicken?

Page 26 Exercise D

Answer the questions with any vocabulary you wish.

Ex. What should I do?

1. What were they talking about?
2. Why is John angry?
3. When does the concert begin?
4. Where are they going to live?
5. How did your sister hurt herself?
6. When will dinner be ready?
7. How old is your grandfather?
8. Where did you put your glasses?
9. How much longer can you stay?
10. When did Bill leave the party?

Page 30 Exercise G

Listen and complete the sentences.

Ex. Will my car be ready today?

1. Is the train on time?
2. Has Jane arrived yet?
3. Did Sam call the doctor?
4. Was the robber arrested?
5. Are you going to see a movie?
6. Does Alan like to dance?
7. Will my father be home soon?
8. Can you visit us tomorrow?
9. Did anyone take out the garbage?
10. Is it going to rain?

Page 43 Exercise J

Listen and complete the sentences.

1. How do you feel . . .
2. Does Tommy still . . .
3. May I borrow this . . .
4. I don't need . . .
5. I'm going to leave . . .
6. They'll be living . . .
7. Arnold is sleeping late because he's . . .
8. I'm sorry you didn't like the salad. It . . .
9. I know they're going to fit . . .
10. My wife and I are taking a few days off next week. We'll . . .
11. I'll try to finish these . . .
12. This week . . .
13. We're leaving . . .
14. Are you going to see your old friends when you're rich . . .
15. I don't think those boys steal . . .
16. You should fill . . .
17. They don't feed . . .
18. George is glad his . . .
19. They're going to get married when they reach . . .
20. I'm glad you liked the pie. Eat . . .
21. We can't fix the TV by ourselves. Will . . .
22. We're going to leave . . .

130

Page 46 Exercise C

Listen and complete the sentences.

Ex. Where are my keys?

1. Where did you put the newspaper?
2. Have my friends arrived yet?
3. Why does your sister want to go home?
4. Is there any homework tonight?
5. What did we do in English class last week?
6. Were Mom and Dad upset this morning?

Page 47 Exercise B

Listen and complete the sentences.

1. If it rains this weekend, . . .
2. I'll have dessert if . . .
3. We'll be late for work if . . .
4. If they finish their homework soon, . . .
5. If our car doesn't start tomorrow morning, . . .
6. If you don't come to class next Monday, . . .
7. She'll be sorry if . . .
8. If Charlie doesn't get a raise soon, . . .
9. I'll call you later if . . .
10. Lois will pick up her husband at the airport if . . .
11. If the children don't feel any better, . . .
12. We won't go on vacation if . . .

Page 80 Exercise K

Listen and complete the sentences.

1. I wish I knew my neighbors. If I knew my neighbors, . . .
2. I hope we're having steak for dinner tonight. If we're having steak for dinner, . . .
3. I wish my brother didn't get into so many fights. If he didn't get into so many fights, . . .
4. I wish my daughter were interested in science. If she were interested in science, . . .
5. I hope Susan is at school today. If she's at school, . . .
6. I wish I lived near a bus stop. If I lived near a bus stop, . . .

Page 80 Exercise L

Listen and complete the sentences.

1. William isn't feeling very well. I wish . . .
2. I didn't understand yesterday's English lesson. I hope . . .
3. My best friend just moved to Centerville. I wish . . .
4. Alice hates working at Ted's Garage. She hopes . . .
5. I'm sorry. I don't know how to swim. I wish . . .
6. I'll try not to step on your feet. I wish . . .
7. We're having a party this weekend. I hope . . .
8. Norman lost his English book. I wish . . .
9. I'm making an apple pie for dessert. I hope . . .
10. My sister is a terrible cook. I wish . . .
11. Our TV is broken. I hope . . .
12. Sheila's used car has been giving her a lot of trouble. She wishes . . .
13. We don't have any onions. I hope . . .
14. I've forgotten Philip's address. I wish . . .

Page 81 Exercise N

Listen and complete the sentences.

1. This morning, I met . . .
2. They fell . . .
3. A tailor . . .
4. There isn't enough pepper . . .
5. Are you Fred . . .
6. Have they made . . .
7. The men . . .
8. We're going to shake . . .
9. My daughter's wedding . . .
10. I need some more paper . . .
11. John's neighbor . . .
12. I'm going to work as a teller . . .
13. Katherine's paid . . .
14. I'll check . . .
15. I don't want to go to school because I fail . . .
16. Mary's pet . . .
17. We have to hurry because Peter's waiting . . .
18. Roger's never . . .
19. Have you seen the Main . . .
20. I'm afraid . . .

Page 83 Exercise D

Listen and complete the sentences.

Ex. My daughter just moved to New York. I wish . . .

1. Martha caught a bad cold. I hope . . .
2. The weather in Honolulu is beautiful. I wish . . .
3. I've forgotten Sarah's address. I hope . . .
4. This is a very difficult math problem. I wish . . .
5. Our apartment isn't big enough. I hope . . .
6. George is taking an important exam tomorrow. He wishes . . .
7. My granddaughter is going skiing this weekend. I wish . . .
8. The concert is going to begin at 7:00. We hope . . .

Page 90 Exercise C

Listen and complete the sentences.

1. My son wants to be a dentist.
2. My brother was chosen "employee of the month."
3. I'm your new mailman.
4. David has been hired by the Ajax Company.
5. I work in that high-rise building across the street.
6. My grandfather just celebrated his 90th birthday.
7. My daughter is finishing college next May.
8. Our neighbors will be moving to Honolulu next week.
9. You're driving me crazy!
10. My little sister can speak four languages fluently.
11. My wife is going to become the manager of our company.
12. My aunt and uncle are going to Rome on their next vacation.
13. Tom was in a terrible car accident and broke his leg.
14. Betty went to Hollywood and was offered a movie contract.
15. Grandma took drum lessons when she was younger.
16. I can't eat ice cream because I'm allergic to milk.

Page 104 Exercise D

Listen and complete the sentences.

Ex. a. You live on Central Avenue . . .
b. You aren't leaving . . .

1. We don't need any more onions . . .
2. You returned your library books . . .
3. Your aunt and uncle are arriving at 3:00 . . .
4. Your brother hasn't cleaned his room yet . . .
5. Your sister was invited to the wedding . . .
6. Your parents just bought a new car . . .
7. She's a professional musician . . .
8. We won't have time to cook a big dinner tonight . . .
9. We can go to the movies this afternoon . . .
10. You'll be home before 10:00 . . .
11. You weren't angry at me this morning . . .
12. He's been a Republican all his life . . .

Page 117 Exercise D

Listen and complete the sentences.

1. He's going to sail . . .
2. If you give me the letter, . . .
3. I need a good lock . . .
4. We're going to heat . . .
5. My foot . . .
6. Peter's bad . . .
7. Ellen said . . .
8. I wish the boss . . .
9. Sarah's caught . . .
10. My uncle's bought . . .
11. I want . . .
12. The policeman's gun . . .
13. My sister's coat . . .
14. The bus hasn't arrived yet . . .
15. I won't . . .
16. David's food . . .
17. Have you seen the ladder . . .
18. You don't have to hit . . .

Page 125 Exercise J

Read the questions and then listen to the passage. Then answer the questions.

JANE'S PROBLEM

When I was unhappy with my job last month, my friend told me not to complain to her. She said I should tell my boss how I felt. I decided to take my friend's advice.

I made an appointment with my boss, and I told him why I didn't like my job. My boss listened quietly for a while, and then he told me why he wasn't satisfied with my work. He said I worked much too slowly, I made too many mistakes, and I complained too much. He told me he thought we'd both be happier if I worked someplace else.

I'm sorry I listened to my friend's advice. If I hadn't listened to my friend's advice, I wouldn't have been fired and I wouldn't be out of work right now.

JENNIFER AND NORMAN

I started going out with Norman when I was a teenager. We fell in love with each other when we were in high school. When I was 25 years old, Norman asked me to marry him, and I accepted.

My parents urged me not to marry Norman. They told me if I married Norman, I'd always regret it. They said he wasn't serious enough, and he would never be successful.

I'm glad I didn't follow my parents' advice, and so are they. Norman and I have been married for 20 years, and we've been very happy. Norman has a good job, and he's a wonderful husband and father.

Our sons are teenagers now, and my parents are a little concerned about them because they aren't serious enough. But I'm not worried about my sons at all because they're just like their father used to be.

Page 126 Exercise M

Listen and complete the sentences.

1. When are you going to wash . . .
2. You're right.
3. Someday . . .
4. Is your bedroom wide . . .
5. I'm going to write . . .
6. My answer is long.
7. They've just rung . . .
8. Your boys . . .
9. This coat hasn't been warm . . .
10. That's light.
11. It's time to watch . . .
12. Have you hurt . . .
13. Our dining room is white . . .
14. I hate chopping . . .
15. My brother's voice . . .
16. My parents send me . . .
17. Sally blushed . . .
18. I always shop . . .
19. I've heard . . .
20. Why haven't you written . . .
21. William always brushes . . .
22. This coat was worn . . .

Page 129 Exercise E

Listen and complete the sentences.

Ex. My son wants to be a doctor.

1. I took ballet lessons when I was younger.
2. My sister drives a school bus.
3. My daughter is going to finish college next year.
4. My wife has been accepted to Greenville College.
5. Bob was in a car accident and broke his arm.

CORRELATION KEY

Student Text Pages	Activity Workbook Pages
Chapter 1	
2–3	1–2 (Exercise A)
4–5	2–4 (Exercises B, C, D, E)
6–7	5–7
10–11	8
15	9–10
Chapter 2	
18–19	11–15
20–21	16
24–25	17
26–27	18–20
Check-Up Test	21–22
Chapter 3	
32	23
33	24–26 (Exercises B, C, D)
34–35	26–28 (Exercise E)
38–39	29–30
42–43	31–32
Chapter 4	
46	33–34
49	35–36
50–51	37–39
52–53	40
54–55	41–44
Check-Up Test	45–46
Chapter 5	
60	47
61	48–50
62–63	51–52
66–67	53–54
68–69	55–57
71	58–59

Student Text Pages	Activity Workbook Pages
Chapter 6	
74–75	60–62
76	63–64
78	65–66 (Exercise E)
79–80	66 (Exercise F)
82	67–68
Chapter 7	
86–87	69–71 (Exercises A, B)
88–89	71–74 (Exercises C, D, E, F, G)
92–93	75–77 (Exercise H)
96–97	77–81 (Exercises I, J, K, L, M, N)
Check-Up Test	82–83
Chapter 8	
100–101	84–88 (Exercise A)
102–103	88–91 (Exercises B, C)
106–108	91–93 (Exercise D)
110–112 top	94–97 (Exercises E, F)
112 bottom	97–100 (Exercises G, H, I)
Chapter 9	
116	101–102
117	103–104
118–119	105
120–121	106–107
122–123	108–109 (Exercises G, H)
128–129	109–111 (Exercises I, J)
Chapter 10	
132–133	112–113
134–135	114–119 (Exercises B, C, D, E)
138–139	119–120 (Exercise F)
140–141	121–125 (Exercises G, H, I)
142–143	125–127 (Exercises J, K, L, M)
Check-Up Test	128–129

Note: A Correlation Key for this workbook may also be found in the Appendix of the *Side by Side* Core Conversation Course—Intermediate Level.